John Mill

The Ottomans in Europe

Or, Turkey in the present crisis, with the secret societies' maps

John Mill

The Ottomans in Europe
Or, Turkey in the present crisis, with the secret societies' maps

ISBN/EAN: 9783337299255

Printed in Europe, USA, Canada, Australia, Japan

Cover: Foto ©ninafisch / pixelio.de

More available books at **www.hansebooks.com**

THE OTTOMANS IN EUROPE;

OR,

TURKEY IN THE PRESENT CRISIS,

WITH THE SECRET SOCIETIES' MAPS.

BY

JOHN MILL,

Author of "Disraeli the Author, Orator, and Statesman;" "Primary, Industrial, and Technical Education," "What is Technical Education?" "A National Technical University," etc., etc.

"If thou, O Lord, art not angry, I am safe: I seek refuge in the light of thy countenance alone."—*Exclamation of Mohammed when stoned out of Tayif.*

LONDON:
WELDON & CO., WINE OFFICE COURT, FLEET STREET.

1876.

[*The Right of Translation is Reserved.*]

CONTENTS.

PRELIMINARY NOTICE.

THE OMLADINA AND PANSLAVONIC MAPS—Their history and purpose—Objects of the Secret Societies—Russia's method of teaching her language—Panslavism and Civilisation.

BOOK I.

THE EASTERN QUESTION.

CHAPTER I.—INTRODUCTION.—Reasons for writing the book: To give a lucid statement of the Eastern Question—Justice to the Turk—Mr. Gladstone and the Prince of Servia—In Asia, England and Turkey stand or fall together ... ... p. 1

CHAPTER II.—THE EASTERN QUESTION—Life or death to the Turk—They will not leave Europe—The field of blood—The Fenians of the East ... ... p. 12

CHAPTER III—RUSSIA AND THE EASTERN QUESTION—Russia's dreams of conquest—Bitterness of Russian life—Poverty of the nation—The intolerable burden of her army.
p. 20

CHAPTER IV.—ENGLAND AND THE EASTERN QUESTION—Our Empire in the East—India—Our foes in the East—Russian efforts to destroy our prestige ... . p. 27

CHAPTER V.—THE EASTERN QUESTION IN AUSTRIA AND THE PRINCIPALITIES—Statecraft—Count Andrassy's "hedging"—Position of Austria in relation to Turkey and to Panslavism—The Montenegrins the Red Indians of Europe—Servia, and the Serbs ... ... p. 31

CHAPTER VI.—SECRET SOCIETIES—Names and objects of the Political Secret Societies of Europe—Objects of the Omladina—The Imperial Panslavonic Societies; their relation to the Magyars, Turks and Germans; their sanguinary objects ... ... p. 38

CHAPTER VII.—RUSSIAN HOPES AND PURPOSES—The Empress a Panslavist—His Imperial Majesty hen-pecked—Ethnological meeting at Moscow; speeches of their Majesties, Prince Gortchakoff, and others—General Fadéef's plan for invading Turkey—Origin of Panslavism—Number of Slavs in Europe ... ... p. 45

CHAPTER VIII.—THE TURK AND THE SLAV—The Osmanli a new race of mankind—The Turk in Europe; his conquests; takes the sword of Islam—The Englishman of the East—The Slav old; Nature's great failure—Cowardice and weakness of the Slav ... ... p. 62

CHAPTER IX.—ISLAM—Character of Mohammedism; its rise and progress—The unlettered prophet—Mahomet takes Elijah as his pattern—Character of the army that invaded Syria; the conquests and its results ... p. 75

BOOK II.

BULGARIAN AND OTHER ATROCITIES.

CHAPTER I.—RAISING OF THE CURTAIN—The Turk to be sacrificed—The Executioners—History of the conspiracy—Brigands in the field—No Christian blood shed in the first encounters ... ... p. 91

CHAPTER II.—THE PLOT THICKENS—The insurgents never tell the truth—Truthfulness and justice of the Turk—The bell grievance—"Brigands, jail-birds, and gipsies" form the Army of Patriots (?)—Policy of the rebels ... p. 99

CONTENTS.

CHAPTER III.—THE CHIEF ACTORS ON THE STAGE—Diplomacy "Bleeding Turkey to death"—The Andrassy Note—End of the farce—The Montenegrins cut off 800 Turkish noses—Russia pays the operators... ... ... p. 109

CHAPTER IV.—KISSING AND SMITING—Duplicity of Turkey's foes—Russia, Austria, Montenegro, Servia, the insurgents, and brigands, all profess love for the Sultan—Number of the insurgent force—The Bulgarian and other massacres planned—Speech of Prince Milan ... ... p. 118

CHAPTER V.—PREPARATIONS FOR MAY-DAY, 1876—A black day—A religious war—Progress of the Turkish Fenians—Preaching of the "hodjis" in the pay of Russia—The sickle of death ... ... p. 128

CHAPTER VI.—BULGARIAN AND OTHER ATROCITIES—The whole planned by the Panslavists—Russian agents—Panslavist schemes—Russian reports of the outrages—Mr. Schuyler's report—The authors of the atrocities—Witnesses against Schuyler—*Levant Herald*—Character of the revolt
p. 135

CHAPTER VII.—BULGARIAN AND OTHER ATROCITIES, CONTINUED —Number of the slain—Edib Effendi and Mr. Baring's reports—Return of the fugitives—Trial of the murderers. —Origin of the atrocities—Mr. Baring condemns Schuyler —Raika, her history and treatment—"Bosh"—Benefit of clergy—Christian girl given to a soldier for his wages—The impalements; exposure of falsehoods ... p. 153

CHAPTER VIII.—BULGARIAN AND OTHER ATROCITIES, CONTINUED Russian atrocities in Central Asia—Kauffman's slaughter of the Turkomans—"Kill them all"—Captain Burnaby's report —Further Russian atrocities in Poland—Siberia and Russian cruelty—American atrocities—General Sheridan and the Indians ... ... p. 173

CHAPTER IX.—THE SERVIAN WAR—Object of the war—General Tchernaieff, agent of the Secret Societies, visits Servia;

his report; his character—Delusions dispelled—Servian cowardice and Turkish valour—Disgrace of Prince Milan—Tchernaieff in disgrace ... ... p. 191

BOOK III.

THE SOLUTION OF THE EASTERN QUESTION.

CHAPTER I.—THE SOLUTION OF THE EASTERN QUESTION—How it must be solved—In Russia, not Turkey—A great surgical operation—Russians and Germans—Fate of the Russian peasantry—Doctrines of the Nihilists and "Old Believers—Russian money-lenders—The land of hatreds—Russia's weakness—The land of corruption—Central Asia—The Sea of Aral—Ambition and impotence. p. 215

CHAPTER II.—CAN THE EASTERN QUESTION BE SOLVED BY REFORMS DEMANDED OF TURKEY?—Reforms demanded on purpose that they should not be acceded to—Peculiar position of Turkey—Capitulations—Consular courts—Taxation—The charter of Turkish liberty ... p. 233

CHAPTER III.—REFORMS DEMANDED BY THE SECRET SOCIETIES—The ghosts of the cabinet councils—Berlin Memorandum—Demand of the insurgents—A revolutionary hen—A joint-stock company, limited—The banditti have "caught a Tartar" ... ... p. 246

CHAPTER IV.—HAVE THE LIBERAL PARTY AN EASTERN POLICY? Is there such a party?—Lord Beaconsfield at the Guildhall—Mr. Gladstone's ravings—"The People's William" in wrath—He discovers a new race—On prayers for the destruction of the Turk—His new definition of "nothing"—War and its horrors—What Mr. Gladstone means—His speech at Staindrop.—Political Holloway's pills—Mr. Lowe and the Duke of Argyll ... ... p. 254

CHAPTER V.—OUR EASTERN POLICY—Our position in Asia—
Our road to India—Mussulmans in India—Trying position
of Lord Derby—His policy—Turkey hardly dealt with—
Signs of the coming times—Turkey and Russia contrasted
—England's Eastern perils ... ... p. 270

APPENDIX ... ... p. 283

PRELIMINARY NOTICE.

THE MAPS given in this work were got up by two distinct parties. The first is that of the OMLADINA,* or Republican branch of the Slavs; the other is IMPERIAL and RUSSIAN, both in its conception and purpose. There are several other maps of a similar kind in circulation, but those given in this work are the most characteristic of the aspirations of the Slavs.

I first became acquainted with the Omladina map in 1856, when a Polish gentleman—a native, I believe, of Warsaw—visited Paris, London, and other large cities, for the purpose of lecturing to his countrymen and others who took an interest in the subject, on Panslavism, which was then a new word to me. He believed, one might also say lived, in his map. There it was, and the work to be done was foreshadowed in it! Being asked when and how it

---

* The word Omladina means youth, and also the after-grass. It is intended here to express the rejuvenescense of the Slavs.

could be accomplished, his reply was, "When the Slav shall arise in his might!"

There is a curious idiosyncrasy in nearly all the members of the political Secret Societies that I have fallen in with, whether they are Irish, French, German, Polish, Italian, or Russian, and I have known some of each nationality. It is, they can believe in the incredible, and are always ready to attempt the impossible. This Polish gentleman, learned, polite, and in other matters seemingly far-seeing, was almost impatient at any suggestion of difficulties in the way of establishing his Republic. Would Russia permit it? What could Russia do to prevent it? Her population was Slav, and must support the Slavs or perish as an Empire. What would Austria do? Austria was a piece of patchwork, sewn together with burning thread; a touch would dissolve that. And Germany, what would she do? Germany was a brute, and must be tamed. It may be remarked that Panslavism was born of hatred to the German race.

All this was said with an intensity of feeling which showed that the speaker was not only an enthusiastic propagandist, but was ready to exchange the pen for the sword whenever the opportunity offered itself.

The second map is Russian, and represents the aspirations of Panslavism as taught by the Secret Societies at Moscow. It owes its origin in its present form to some remarks made by the Empress (see Book I, chapter vii.), that were addressed to a deputation which waited upon her, "when," the report says, "Her Majesty deigned to express her regret that the varied Slavonian races had not a common alphabet and orthography." The loyal *savants* took the matter into consideration and resolved that Russian should be the common language of the Slavs, wherever they are found.

Before this ethnographical maps had been circulated, which showed the distribution of the Slav population marked in special colours. This map was improved, or rather altered, to show in what districts it was desirable the Russian language should be taught. In the first maps light patches appeared indicating the existence of Magyars, Turks, and other races. This, however, was discontinued after a while, since it had been determined to dispose of those races altogether. The Omladina were to subdue the Magyars, the Panslavists were to drive the Turks out of Europe, the Germans also were to be sent back to Germany Proper; hence the map was amended, and sent out privately by "those whom you know" to the Panslavonic committees.

Absurd as all this may seem—more, indeed, like the dream of a madman or fanatic than the thoughts of a politician or statesman—still it is an event in contemporary history. It is now the day-dream of millions; but Russia has already drilled and armed one million two hundred and fifty thousand men, and she will shortly have double that number, each with a breech-loader in his hand and cartridges in his pouch to make the dream this map suggests a terrible reality.

The Panslavists tell us that theirs is a purely ethnographical map, showing where the common language of the Slavs has to be taught. Russia's method of teaching her language is simple and characteristic. She builds no schools nor colleges, but makes it a criminal offence to speak any language but her own, and visits with fine and imprisonment all who dare to speak their native tongue. She has been keeping school in this fashion for some years past in Poland, and desires now to extend the benefit of her educational system to the whole of Eastern Europe; or, to use Mr. Baring's words, "to break up the Austrian and Turkish Empires."

Down to the commencement of 1875 Panslavism had been little other than a game of brag and vapid boasting. There had, it is true, been a more liberal use of the knout on the Roman Catholic Christians in Poland, but that was all. It may be said to have commenced its first operations in the field in getting up the so-called Herzegovinian insurrection; then the Bulgarian atrocities (see Book II., chaps. 1, 2, 3), and the Montenegrian and Servian wars. All this was done THAT A RUSSIAN

FORCE SHOULD, IF POSSIBLE, GET POSSESSION OF THE PASSES OF THE BALKANS without a declaration of war. That is the "MATERIAL GUARANTEE" which Russian statesmen are now talking about for the carrying out of the reforms in Turkey A LA POLOGNE.

At the time when the Panslavists began their bad work, last year, there was peace, contentment, and general prosperity throughout the Turkish Empire. In comparison with the best portions of Russia, the Christian people were better fed, clothed, sheltered, and governed, paid less taxes, and enjoyed a degree of civil and religious liberty unknown beyond the Pruth. They were exempt from military service, and, to crown all, ten times as well educated as the Russian peasantry are. It is the misfortune of Europe, as well as that of the Russian soldier, that there is no place so bad as his own home. Hence the insatiable longing for the sunny vales and fertile plains of Eastern Europe and Asia Minor.

The first year of the Panslavists' active operations closed with this result: the desolation of Herzegovina and a portion of Bulgaria, and the ruin of Servia. The needless sacrifice of tens of thousands of lives: the ruin, indeed, of the Christian people who they professed to help. These are its first fruits. What the great harvest of death will be, before its evil work is done, appals the mind to contemplate.

PANSLAVISM is the great fact for European statesmen to consider. It has taken the field in open arms against treaties, races, religions, culture—in one word, CIVILISATION, as understood in Western Europe. The question is, which will conquer?

LONDON,
  8th December, 1876.

BOOK I.

THE EASTERN QUESTION.

BOOK I.

CHAPTER I.

INTRODUCTION.

For some time past it has been my intention to publish a work on the Races, Religions and Resources of the Ottoman Empire, in which what is technically called the EASTERN QUESTION would have had a very subordinate place. The force of events has, however, caused a deviation from this course, and hence this volume is confined mainly to the present Crisis.

Two objects have been kept constantly in view in the composition of this book.

The first was to prepare a full and lucid statement of the Eastern Question, and everything immediately pertaining to it down to the time of going to press, and to deduce that statement mainly from parliamentary documents. Comparatively little use has been made of newspaper reports. Not that they are not worthy of credence. They are, indeed, the productions of able and conscientious men, who do their work with a heroism and fidelity beyond all praise. They watch the *dénouement* of the plot as it is unfolded on the stage, and judge the actors by their performances; but they see little of the playwrights, stage-managers and property-men, who are usually in the background, and it is with them principally that the Blue Books deal.

It must be confessed that though they are the best of books they are not usually the most lively reading, and hence a BLUE BOOK has almost passed into a proverb for dulness. This really is not the case, and it is the form in which it is presented rather than the matter which they contain, that renders them uninviting. Our Diplomatic and Consular Service is in the hands of men of the highest character and ability, and what they write is usually worth reading, and may be taken as the most accurate view of the subject that can, at the time of writing, be obtained.

There is another advantage in writing contemporary history from Blue Books,—namely, that they are easy of access and convenient for reference; hence, if a mistake is made by any Consul or other writer at a particular time and place, it is sure to be corrected either by himself or some one else, and thus we have something like an accurate statement of facts, and not coming from one single place but from places scattered over vast empires, all throwing light upon one particular series of events.

The Eastern Question, then, as spoken of in this book, is the Eastern Question as it has come before our Ambassadors and Consuls, and has been presented by them to our Government ever since the first attempt to get up an insurrection in Herzegovina. It will therefore, it is hoped, form a useful compendium of facts and references for those who may not agree with the author in some of the opinions which are advanced.

Again, this is an attempt to do justice to the Turk and defend him against his traducers. The defence will, however, be seen to be in the facts as they are unfolded in the narrative, and not in any special pleading in his behalf. Indeed, if the facts will not defend him the case is hopeless. At present the public has only heard the counsel for the prosecution. The case for the defendant has not yet been even opened in any popular and condensed form that I am aware of, and it is this case, or rather a section of it, which will be found in the following pages.

I defend the Turk as I would defend a young and noble brother whose education has been neglected, and who had unhappily fallen into bad hands. In such a case the mantle of charity should be thrown over his minor misdeeds; his more serious offences admitted and atoned for, if possible. And then, "as in the course of justice none of us should see salvation," I should ask, is he a greater sinner than all else? Where is the clean hand that shall cast the first stone at him? The reader will find something upon this point when we come to speak of Bulgarian and other atrocities.

Compared to the Jew, Arab, Greek and Hindoo, and even the Celt, the Turk is very young. In the first flush of youth he went forth to conquer, and having won a large estate, like many another prodigal son spent much of it in riotous living. He was, however, as rudely awakened as Samson was from his sleep in the house of Delilah. It was not only that the Philistines were upon him, the body-snatchers were ready to bear him to the dissecting-room and have him cut up that they might divide the carcase between them.

Twenty-five years ago he was held to be the "Sick Man," ready to die. Now he is so strong that if not killed soon the task will be impossible. Hence the gathering of the bloodthirsty Slavs in Servia. As Homer says:—

> "A grim, terrific, formidable band:
> Grim as voracious wolves who seek the springs,
> When scalding thirst their burning bowels wrings;
> When some tall stag, fresh slaughter'd in the wood,
> Has drench'd their wide insatiate throats with blood;
> To the black font they rush, a hideous throng,
> With paunch distended and with lolling tongue,
> Fire fills their eyes, their black jaws belch the gore,
> And gorged with slaughter, still they thirst for more."

What has the Turk done to them that they should come to rob, and murder, and deluge some of the fairest provinces of Europe with blood? Even Mr. Gladstone is obliged to admit that the Servian " HAD NO STATEABLE CAUSE OF WAR." And he adds this astounding assertion: "It does not follow that she has committed a wanton aggression, *or has, in fact, been guilty of any moral offence.*" Such a doctrine, coming from such a quarter, almost takes one's breath away! What does the right honourable gentleman mean?

The Prince of Servia is the sworn vassal of the Sultan, bound by every tie that high heaven can sanction. He never asked to be, nor ever was absolved from his oath by his lawful sovereign. Has perjury ceased to be a crime? May princes' be "like dicer's oaths, false as hell," and the Prince still be free from all moral offence?

Again, as Byron says, "War's a brain-spattering, windpipe-splitting art, unless her cause by RIGHT is sanctified." Servia invaded Turkey without "any stateable cause of war," and began to rob and murder. Was there no moral offence in that? If not the brand on Cain was evidently a mistake. He ought to have been a Servian General, and have been decorated for his deed.

By every Religion that men have ever believed in in this world, or hoped to be saved by in the next; by every system of morality that sages have taught, and the nobler and purer instincts of humanity have followed; by every code or law of honour that has been recognised by people calling themselves civilised; is this outrage on the Turks condemned, and is judged accursed by God and man.

It is only fair to the Panslavists to say that if there be degrees in their hatred they detest the English a little more than they do the Turks. They see what the great mass of our people and some of our statesmen have not yet realised, THAT IN ASIA, ENGLAND AND TURKEY STAND OR FALL TOGETHER. The funeral knell, which booms out its solemn note over the grave of the Turk, will be the signal for our expulsion from India.

On every ground then, of truth, justice, honour, and national interest, I defend the Turk. How far I have done so successfully will be seen in the following pages.

CHAPTER II.

THE EASTERN QUESTION.

WHAT, then, is "this interminable Eastern Question," as Lord Derby calls it? Put it to the leading statesmen of seven great nations, and the probability is that you will get a different answer from each of them, especially if they should say what they mean.

In its broad and general form it is: Supposing the Turk were to die, be killed, or hopelessly conquered, how shall his property be disposed of?

Now as the Turk does not intend to die, or be killed, or conquered either if he can help it, the diplomatists are much in the position of the amiable people whom Dickens represents as meeting at the house of Mr. Pecksniff to dispose of the estate and effects of a certain gentleman who suddenly got well and left them to wrangle.

To the Turk it means Life or Death, Existence or Dissolution, and he accepts it with all its terrible consequences. With him, "To be or not to be? That is the question."

He has been where he is for centuries. His fathers won the inheritance for him with their blood and valour, in fairly contested battle-fields, led there, as he firmly believes, by a Divine Providence that never errs. He is not appalled by all the hosts that may be brought against him. They can only give him martyrdom. Allah, the All Merciful, has placed him where he is, and it matters little to him whether he yields up his spirit to the Beneficent One who gave it, a few days earlier or later.

The Turk then will not go; neither will he live a serf in the land which he once governed. He is like Kaled, whom the Prophet called "The Sword of Allah," who, being opposed by a host, ten times as numerous as his own, cut his way through the hostile ranks, his little army, says the historian, looking "like a white spot on the back of a black camel." Being asked by the Caliph why he ran such risk rather than retreat, he replied, "I was afraid that God would see me turn my back." God nor man will ever see the Turk turn his back on the fair possessions and holy places committed to his charge.

We ask those gentlemen who talk so glibly about driving the Turks out of Europe, to think of the consequences involved in this exploit. They are to go " one and all, bag and baggage," says Mr. Gladstone. But they will no more go than Mr. Gladstone will go out of his possessions at the mandate of the first

Communists who tell him and his to go "bag and baggage, and leave his estates to the people."

At the Guildhall meeting some of the speakers not only advocated the expulsion of the Turks from Europe, but there were loud cries for " Gladstone" to come and order them off. Well, let us suppose the right honourable gentleman to be again Prime Minister of Great Britain, with Earl Russell and the Duke of Argyll as members of his cabinet, and we will suppose also, for humanity's sake, that they will not " meddle and muddle," as they did in the Crimean war, when they sent as brave and noble an army as ever left our shores since the first " silver host" of the Triads, to die of cold, and hunger, and disease, until Balaclava and the camps above became a hell of agony, and it is almost as much as hoping that the Ethiopian will change his skin and the leopard his spots; but having supposed it, here is the little task which they have before them.

They have more people to " remove"—that is, starve or kill, for in this case they prefer removal to another world to subjection and degradation in this— than form the whole population of the kingdoms of Holland, Denmark, and Greece; more by nearly two millions than make up the inhabitants of Scotland; a million more than the entire Roman Catholics of Ireland ; more, indeed, than the whole population of Belgium ; so that if every man, woman, and child were swept out of that " cock-pit of Europe," it would not equal the "removal" of the Turks, "one and all, bag and baggage,"* from their homes and heritage in Europe.

The human mind fails to realise such an Aceldama. "The field of blood" is too vast for any range but that of a demon's vision. As the Slavs, Cossacks, and Calmucks advance they will pass over ravaged fields, burnt villages, and ruined towns. Fair cities, like Adrianople and Philippopolis, will be razed to the ground. It will be a conflict for dear life, and whatever else the Turk may do he will "die hard." The insurgent chiefs of Herzegovina have just informed the courts of Europe that they intend to fight it out to the "bitter end." The end means desolation—the fair provinces of Eastern Europe a howling wilderness. Even those bandits will not be able to live in the country; the industrious and honest people being gone, their infernal calling will be at an end: the wolves will have devoured their last sheep.

And all this time there will be slaughter in battles such as the world has, let us hope, never seen. As the starving Slav advances over the desolated earth he will find a battery of Krupp's artillery in every mountain gorge. The breachloader will rain its

---

* I am sorry to see that some who use the language referred to say they only meant official personages. Then why not say so at once? Their friends, the Russians, mean to sweep the land with "the besom of destruction."

death-storm, the bayonet pierce, and the sabre cleave. No quarter will be asked for or given. It will be a war of RACE and RELIGION. A war to the knife and to the death.

The numbers engaged in that conflict would be immense. If the Panslavists are let alone by Austria, England, and the other Powers, and backed by Russia, they can bring three hundred thousand soldiers into the field; whether they could feed and sustain them is doubtful—certainly not for any length of time without external aid; and if the Turks can prolong the struggle beyond the Balkans for two years, which they can do, they can bring an equal, if not larger number, to the scene of action. We shall speak of the Turkish army in another chapter; we speak here simply of the prime element in an army—MEN.

The number of men which may be available for Turkey, if the extreme crisis which now seems inevitable be forced upon her, must not be calculated by what is technically called the population of the Turkish Empire. The Sultan is the head, not only of his Empire, but of Islam. Two hundred million souls look to him *as holding for them* the sword of Othman. They are of many *varieties* and *races* of mankind—Caucasian, Mongolian, Malay, and Ethiopian; black, white, copper-coloured, and tawny. But they are one Brotherhood; and in the sight of Allah " there is no high, no low, no great, no small." The beggar in the lazar-house and the Sultan in his palace are all one in HIS presence.

The Sultan holds for them also, in the name of all "true believers," many of the most holy places in the world. The Holy Land is all theirs, and he holds it in trust for them, and must guard every foot of it from Dan to Beersheba. The Dead Sea, that monument of Divine displeasure; Mount Carmel, where the idolators were confuted; and, above all, Jerusalem, the ancient Salem, where Abraham met Melchisedeck, where scores of prophets lived, died, and are buried; where the Temple of Solomon once stood, and from whose site the prophet ascended to the celestial spheres, saw the "eternal blazon," the spirits of just men made perfect, when God had wiped away all tears from their eyes.

Let it be known, then, throughout the Mahometan world, that the chief of Islam is to be assailed, that the true believers are to be slain in millions, that the holy places, won by the valour of the companions of the Prophet, are to be taken from them; for it is absurd to talk of pausing at Constantinople if the Slavs ever get there, and the Mussulmans will come from far and near. Arabia will send clouds of cavalry; every family will give its best and bravest son to the holy war. India, Africa, as well as Europe and Asia Minor, will pour forth their contingents. Their hosts will come as the billows of the sea when the wind blows towards the shore, and everyone that breaks upon the advancing steel of the brutal Slav will be followed by a higher and a fiercer wave.

We have had something like it in Western Europe, when the extinction of Protestantism was determined on by the *Christian* (?) Princes, headed by the Pope. It is the Orthodox Greek instead of the Infallible Latin Church which provokes the slaughter now. They have already created a St. Bartholomew massacre in Bulgaria, and are about to send forth an armed host that will do deeds as dreadful as any that Alva could have perpetrated if he had added to his other brutal campaigns the conquest of England. Even in our own islands we are not without examples. More than one attempt has been made to drive the English out of Ireland, and we all know how Cromwell treated one of those affairs when he, as Carlyle says, abandoned " rose-water surgery." The Fenians tell us they are only waiting for some combination or complication of matters to do the work even now. Well, the Fenians of Eastern Europe have broken loose, and are doing the work of the father who begat them as thoroughly as the monsters who tried to blow down the Clerkenwell House of Detention.

This, then, is the form in which the Eastern Question is propounded to the Turk. It is to his credit that he never raised or suggested it in this fashion. Indeed, he never raised it at all. It is Russia who has been raising and pressing it for so many years past with restless impetuosity, and now it has become a world's question, and the pulses of the great nations of Europe are fast rising to fever-heat upon the subject.

I shall, doubtless, be told that this is an over statement of the case, and that all that is required is that the governing classes of the Turks should go, leaving the weak and quiet to be governed by the Christian population. Mr. Gladstone is very minute and emphatic, and, though repeating a phrase which has been already used, again cite his words. He says:—" An old servant of the Crown and State, I entreat my countrymen, upon whom far more than perhaps any other people of Europe it depends, to require and to insist that our Government, which has been working in one direction, shall work in the other, and shall apply all its vigour to concur with the other States of Europe in obtaining the extinction of the Turkish executive power in Bulgaria. Let the Turks now carry away their abuses in the only possible manner—namely, by carrying off themselves. Their Zaptiehs and their Mudirs, their Bimbashis and their Yuzbachis, their Kaimakams, and their Pashas, one and all, bag and baggage, shall, I hope, clear out from the province."

I suppose no tyrant or "sturdy man-destroying villain who has laid empires waste" ever asked for more. The man of learning, the artist and art workman, the skilled mechanic, the industrious agriculturalist, all but the lowest savages value, and will, if possible, retain them in their dominions. I can easily imagine Nana Sahib sitting over the well at Cawnpore and writing a similar despatch—telling the English to clear out of India, bag and baggage, with their governor-general, councillors, judges, diplomatists, collectors, and soldiers, from the commander-in-chief to the smallest drummer boy. The physicians, surgeons, engineers, chemists, and skilled workmen might remain, they being of immense value everywhere.

But would they go when ordered? Only on the same conditions as the Turks will leave Europe—when the last shot has been fired and the last arm broken that can wield a sabre!

CHAPTER III.

RUSSIA AND THE EASTERN QUESTION.

As remarked in the last chapter, the Eastern Question assumes various forms and colours as it is viewed by different nations. The view which is forced upon Turkey has already been given, not as she could receive, but as she must, if needs be, accept it. She is not asked to surrender a province to round off another kingdom, or to remove some obstruction or hindrance to the peace, prosperity, and commerce of the world as we have often done, and as she might do with honour. The Turk is either not asked to do anything at all, or else, with a cannon pointed at his head, required to perform some impossible thing. We shall see many instances of this as we proceed.

The kaleidoscope, then, as looked into at Constantinople, is red with fire and blood. The view at St. Petersburg is like that presented to those who, after being long in the wilderness, climbed the steep sides of Pisgah and looked down on the promised land. The nations inhabiting it cause little concern—they are "food for powder." But the land is flowing with milk and honey. From their gloomy woods, frozen rivers and lakes, their snow-clad steppes, and barren plains, where the struggle for existence with the demons of the ice and the desert is always keen, they look towards Constantinople as the key to their earthly paradise. The slaughter of the Moslems gives zest to the idea, like a glass of raki before dinner.

In speaking of Russia, however, we must make allowance for her people and their rulers. This earth-hunger is as natural to them as the desire for warmth to those who are cold. More than this, they have drank in this longing for conquest with their mother's milk. From the time of Peter the Great something like a definite plan or scheme has been working out. A glance at the maps that have been published during the last century show some strange alterations in the boundaries of that Empire; but whatever else has been done or left undone, the efforts to reach Constantinople and India have been steadily persisted in.

Russia is a cold, poor country, and the burden of life rests heavily upon the shoulders of nearly the whole population. The short summer has scarcely faded into the autumn before the piercing frost and bitter snow storms set in, and the whole country is ice-bound. It is no wonder that they should dream of, and long for, the sunny south with its balmy air, bright skies, and fertile plains and dales. One might as well tell the hungry not to long for food, and the thirsty for drink, as tell the dwellers in the North not to long for a more genial climate. When the Norwegians were converted to Christianity in the ninth century the King begged the missionaries not to tell his people that the nether regions were hot, or all their converts would want to go there.

The Russians are also a religious people with grand propagandist ideas. Every child learns with its first catechism that Holy Russia has a great mission to perform, and that one of the things which has to be accomplished is the rescue of St. Sophia at Constantinople and the edifice on Mount Moriah from the Turk; and every aspiring youth looks forward, and longs for the time when he shall be a soldier in the army, which shall redeem those places from bondage. We have thus the elements of a bitter death grip. The Russ would die to gain what the Turk would die rather than give up.

The Russian Government has also another source of embarrassment: a ghost which no spell yet discovered can allay. Its presence is felt in the palace; it stalks through the barracks and enters in all its bony nakedness into every house and hovel in the Empire. It is POVERTY. The Empire is miserably poor. Over two hundred millions have been borrowed, and the greater quantity spent upon nonproductive works, principally in constructing and organising a vast army. Even the railways made with English money have been military lines, that yield no revenue to the State, and yet the English bondholders have to be paid.

Many of her conquests have been equally barren of spoil and yield little income to the exchequer, as we shall presently show. What can be obtained from wandering nomads or the poor States of Central Asia? And yet they have cost vast sacrifices both in men and money to conquer, and now it is found cannot be held unless they are connected with Moscow by a railway. Even if made it will only be a military line, and will consequently be an additional burden to the State. But we shall speak of this more fully when we come to discuss *the solution* of the Eastern Question.

Russia is poor, frozen, and land-locked. Her one open port to the ocean in Europe—Archangel—is frozen half the year; the Key to the Baltic is held by another nation, that of the Mediterranean by the Turk. She has the Amoor, it is true, but a fleet at Kamschatka is of little avail in a European contest.

In this condition the country is suffering, ground to the earth, indeed, by her military system; the army is a burden that has become almost too intolerable to be borne, and she sits upon a volcano of secret societies, which may any day cause a convulsion at home or plunge the nation into a foreign war.

Let us first glance at her army.

Russia has recently adopted the system of general compulsory service on the Prussian model, but she has gone farther than Prussia; for the latter keeps her soldiers only three years in the ranks, and four years in the reserve, afterwards passing them into the Landwehr and Landsturm. But Russia keeps them six years in the ranks and nine years in the reserve, thus giving a longer training and eventually a larger reserve; and there can be little doubt that these trained men on leaving the reserve will, as in Prussia, be made available for the defence of the country as long as they remain serviceable. It is calculated that in nineteen years the Russian army will have been raised by this system to nearly 3,000,000 trained soldiers, and this estimate does not include her frontier Cossacks, which number about 400,000 irregular cavalry.

In the course of years, when the Russian Landwehr and Landsturm are formed, this enormous force will be further augmented, and probably 3,000,000 will be available for offensive purposes.

Even at the present moment the numbers composing the Russian army are formidable. The active force which could be placed in the field consists of 500 battalions of infantry and 32 of rifles; 56 regiments of cavalry, 1,040 field guns and 400 mitrailleuse, 11 battalions of sappers, 1 company of Turkestan sappers, 6 half battalions pontooniers, and 6 telegraph parks.

In addition to this force there are 80 reserve

battalions of infantry, 56 squadrons of cavalry, 12 field battalions, 4 horse batteries, 4 battalions of sappers. There are also, besides these, 48 battalions of infantry, and 25 garrison battalions, with 91 companies of garrison artillery, the whole forming a force of ONE MILLION ONE HUNDRED AND THIRTY-EIGHT THOUSAND MEN. Nor is this even all, for there are in addition between three and four hundred thousand Cossacks, not included in the former calculation.

It will thus be seen that the new Russian army organisation is the most fearful embodiment of military power ever attempted by any nation ancient or modern. It involves the principle of universal obligatory service in the 20th year, and about 700,000 youths annually attain this prescribed age. But the State claims the services of every man for twenty years. Deducting 40 per cent. for physical or other unfitness, it leaves 420,000 men annually available. Of these the army only takes into its ranks about 150,000, leaving 270,000 in reserve. Peaceable people have one consolation : it is that this huge force must like a serpent move on its belly. Russia cannot feed it on its march : destroy all before it, and it must perish of hunger and disease.

But in reserve to this terrible force there are the 270,000 annually drawn, but not passed into the ranks, which in twenty years will give an additional strength of 5,400,000, minus losses, only partially trained, like our volunteers, but liable to immediate service.*

The cost of this immense force is now, in time of peace, £30,000,000 a year. What will it be in time of war?

The abstraction of so much of the vital force of the nation from profitable industrial pursuits not only leaves the country poor, but throws the labour upon the weaker portion of the community, with whom there is a bitter struggle for existence. The lads and old men toil like galley slaves, the women dig and delve in fields and quarries, and are even hod carriers, coal and wood porters.

But they all live and toil, and have their energies pressed into the great man-machine, the army, which is one day to work out their emancipation and give them the wealth and luxury of richer countries—of Turkey and India.

Thus they hunger as they groan beneath the load of life, and long for conquests: the devout pray for it; the greedy covet it; the soldiers are held like bloodhounds in a leash while the secret societies are setting fire to the cord.

Russia is boiling her eggs for breakfast in fires which glow and throb from subterranean depths.

---

* See "Clouds in the East," by Col. V. Baker, pp. 357, 358.

CHAPTER IV.

ENGLAND AND THE EASTERN QUESTION.

THE Eastern Question is to us "the burning question" of the day, and is likely to be so for many days to come. It is at present a little obscured by the smoke arising from the Bulgarian atrocities and the dust which Mr. Gladstone and his friends have raised. That, however, will soon clear away. After strict investigation the real truth will be ascertained; the guilty, if possible, punished; the wronged, so far as it can be done, compensated. There will be a blush for our common humanity that such things could be, a tear for the victims, and then the whole matter must be left to HIM who hath numbered the hairs of every head, and never lets a sparrow fall unnoticed. "Think you that the Heaven and the Earth were created in jest?" says the Koran. Nay, all these deeds will be weighed in the Eternal Balances, and woe unto him whose scale is laden with guilt.

The Eastern Question, then, has become an

English Question—we might almost say a party-question; but that, we hope, will not long continue. It has been brought to the hustings and ballot-box once already, and been rightfully decided. Let us hope it was for the first and last time. Mr. Gladstone, as is usual with him, sees three courses.* If the right honourable gentleman could only see a fourth—and that is to forget the wrongs, whatever they may be, which caused him, like Achilles, to retire to his tent, and above all to remember that this great empire was not created specially for party politicians—there might be some hope for him. But we shall discuss this matter when speaking of its solution, and hence proceed to define the Eastern Question as seen from an English point of view.

It will be seen by a reference to that singular document, the will of Peter the Great, that the primary aim put forward in it is directed toward India; and it was evidently conceived by the author, whoever he may have been, in a spirit of antagonism towards England, rather than any other country. And this policy has been carried out. It may be true that there is no present intention of invading India, either through Persia or by any other route. Indeed, so far as I can perceive, after a careful study of the matter, any attempt of the kind would be attended with results as fatal as the invasion of Russia by Napoleon I. Still, why has

---

* See "Bulgarian Horrors," pp. 14, 15.

Russia beggared herself, and wasted so much life in making profitless conquest in Central Asia, if it be not to hold the sword of Damocles over our head in that quarter?

When the Eastern Question, therefore, is presented to an Englishman, the thought which naturally and instinctively arises in his mind may be expressed in one word: it is—INDIA.

Next to his own Island Home, the thing dear to an Englishman is India! HOME is too sacred for discussion. When a Parliamentary Commission sat some years ago to enquire into our National Defences, one of the questions submitted to it was, What should be done in the provinces, supposing London to be in the hands of an invading force? No reply was given—it was an idea too horrible ever to be discussed.

Abana and Pharphar, rivers of Damascus, may in the estimation of the Syrian, be better than all the waters of Israel; but to the true Englishman they are poor and feeble in comparison with the Mersey and the Thames. What Jerusalem is to the Jew, the Caaba to the Mussulman, England is to the true Briton. It is the ark in which the liberty of the world is kept and held secure—in which the manna of religion and science which feeds the free souls of the good is kept unhurt by the curses of priests and the ban of tyrants.

And next to it is India. It is the apple of the

Englishman's eye. We have more than fifty Colonies, some of them great federations of States. Canada itself owns the fifth mercantile navy in the world, both in number of ships and weight of tonnage. But our colonies give us little care or thought: *they cannot go away from us.* We may defy them to dis-Anglicise themselves. They have our language, laws, literature, and religion. They must be Englishmen. Nature has put that stamp upon them, and it can never be effaced. Neither, indeed, has earth anything that could tempt them to leave us. It is a case of mother and filial love, that silver cord cannot be broken.

It is different with India. With her we have no ties, either of race or religion; indeed, those are against us. God has committed to our care a child with a vast inheritance—so ancient, yet so fresh and young; prolific now as it was thousands of years ago; gifted with such noble qualities, yet so weak and ready to become the prey of unscrupulous conquerors. It is a trust which Divine Providence has appointed us to administer, and we cannot give our stewardship to another.

Besides, we are proud of India—it is such a monument of our valour, daring, and administrative ability. When we read of great nations and great states and empires, we smile and think of our own, of which India is the gem. What were the one hundred and twenty-seven provinces of Babylon, or even the Roman Empire itself, in comparison with ours? The English own this day about EIGHT MILLION SQUARE MILES of territory upon the earth's surface, five times more, at least, than Rome ever possessed. In making his estimation of the population of Rome, Gibbon, calculating from the census papers of the Roman citizens by Claudius, assumes the population of the Empire in its palmiest days to be " about a hundred and twenty millions of persons . . . . the most numerous society that has ever been united under the same system of government."* The census of 1871 of the British Empire gives the result, as of actual British subjects, TWO HUNDRED AND THIRTY-FOUR MILLION, SEVEN HUNDRED AND SIXTY-TWO THOUSAND, FIVE HUNDRED AND NINETY-THREE. This, however, does not include those " under British protection " in India and other places, which raises the number above 250,000,000, or fully one-fourth of the human species.

That, then, is our heritage! We are not asked to sell it; for the world, if it cast all its treasures into one lap, could offer no price for it. We are not even like Esau, tempted to sell it for a mess of pottage; for we are fed to repletion, and the food of our poor is better than that of the rich in many countries. Still, there is a wild dream in certain quarters that it may be taken from us.

" Perhaps this was the pate of a politician who

---

* " Roman Empire," chaps. i. and ii.

could circumvent God," says Shakspeare, and it is just that order of beings who would, if it were possible, destroy the British Empire. They scarcely exist in mid Europe. The revolutionists of France, Italy, and Germany regard England as a city of refuge, and they would, if it were necessary, fight to the bitter death for her, and we may add also that the Governments of Western Europe are all equally friendly. France has learned by bitter experience that England is her best friend. Denmark, Holland, and Belgium look up to her as their protector. The Italians are our brothers in freedom and faith, the Germans in blood. We must therefore look to the East for our foes.

And they are there, armed to the teeth, in hundreds of thousands, nay millions. Why has Russia adopted the German system of recruiting her army, and converted the whole population into an arms-bearing people? Certainly not for defensive purposes! I do not believe that Russia has in the whole of her vast empire a single province which anyone would go to war for. If there be an exception to this it is in the provinces which were taken from China not long since, and which the Celestials talk of recovering. In Europe and Central Asia she is quite welcome to all she has.

Why, then, this vast armament? We can scarcely say that the object is concealed. It is to crush Turkey, and take India from England. The Eastern

Question therefore, as seen from London, is, " Shall the English be driven out of India?" And after all that resolves itself into another question: Can Russia frighten or drive us out?

CHAPTER V.

THE EASTERN QUESTION IN AUSTRIA AND THE PRINCIPALITIES.

The existence of Austria, like Turkey, lies in the Eastern Question. The Panslavists make no secret of the matter, since in their programme they dispose of the whole of her territory. With the Omladina, as will be seen by their map, Austria is doomed. To use an American phrase, that Empire is to be "wiped out."

Austria holds a peculiar position in the family of European States. She is the most impalpable of modern nations. Hungary, Bohemia, Transylvania, Croatia, Dalmatia, and a portion of Poland with some other minor places, such as the Tyrol, have hitherto consented to be governed by the House of Hapsburg, and Vienna has thus become the centre of Government for a number of States which have little or no sympathy with, and scarcely any common feeling, except that of antagonism, for each other.

STATECRAFT has always found its home and native air in Austria. "Divide and govern" has been the motto of her statesmen, and has been carried out with a ruthless disregard to anything but the end in view. It must be admitted that the governing idea has generally been wise, and in some cases beneficent. But it never had, nor, so far as I know, ever desired to have, the light of Heaven for its guidance.

It ever has been, and still is, of the earth, earthly. It will make a Concordat with Rome, or break it, with equal indifference; will be despotic, liberal, even Panslavonic, provided its ends be attained. One would, if possible, fain think well of Austria, for she is generally our ally; but in this Turkish affair, as in many others, I find it impossible to do so. As her policy comes out in the Blue Books before us, it is branded with hypocrisy. Count Andrassy appears to have entered on the Eastern Question as certain gamblers known as "bookmakers" go on the turf. Those gentlemen are always "hedging," and will tell you that they stand to win so much upon every possible issue of the event. The Count is the political bookmaker who is always "hedging." He holds with the hare but runs with the hounds, and makes quite sure of being in at the death.

Two or three years ago it was whispered in political

circles that Austria was entitled to some compensation for the loss of her Italian possessions; and not daring so much as to look over the hedge, much less steal a sheep from either Germany or Russia, she turned her eyes on Turkey to see what might be had there. This, as we shall see presently, was the first letting out of the waters of strife.

The position of Austria, in relation to the affairs of Turkey, is very peculiar. She cannot, or at least will not, let matters alone, and she has to enter upon them with her most deadly foes, and without a friend who will help her to any portion of Turkish territory. All the other Powers, excepting Russia, desire to see the Turkish Empire maintained in all its integrity. She cannot therefore look to them for support in any scheme for the annexation of territory, and yet her greed for provinces will not let her rest.

Ever since the Crimean War there has existed in Russia the most bitter hatred and contempt for Austria. She was saved by Russian soldiers in 1848 from utter destruction, and so firmly did the late Emperor believe in her dependence on, and gratitude to him, that he said on one memorable occasion, "What I do, Austria will do." And yet in the hour of Russia's extreme agony she was abandoned. That act of ingratitude will never be forgotten nor forgiven; and hence, should the Panslavists ever succeed in establishing their Republic, they can not only calculate on sympathy from Russia in carrying out their work—at all events while they let her territory alone—but she would be the first to recognise the new State.

The whole, however, is a tangled knot, which no diplomatic cunning is ever likely to untie. Some day or other the sword will cut it.

Austria and Russia had agreed, and we were informed that their unanimity was wonderful; that *some change* must be made in Turkey, or, "not to put too fine a point upon it," each wanted a slice of the noble bird, though they were not quite certain what each should take. A leg and a wing might do for Austria; the Emperor of Russia and "the Old Russian party" would have been content with the breast in the form of an advance of their frontier from the Pruth to the Danube, and a Protectorate over Bulgaria. This scheme was hard to swallow at Vienna; but they were saved the difficult process by a third party claiming not only the whole they were contending for, but much more—nothing less, indeed, than a PANSLAVONIC REPUBLIC or a PANSLAVIC EMPIRE, as shown in our Maps; and that Turkey in Europe and Austria, as a State, should cease to exist.

In the meantime, however, each had been doing a little diplomatic business in its own way. As in playing chess, the game was opened with pawns. Austria opened with Montenegro, and made her first move. This was replied to by Russia, who advanced Servia as a counter-move. It was never intended, however, that this should be a game of pawns. Still, before relating the progress of events, we may as well see what those minor pieces on the board are.

The Montenegrins inhabit a hilly and mountainous district, almost inaccessible, not very large, and miserably poor. Every man is esteemed to be a soldier, but the privates have no pay. They are, indeed, supposed to live on plunder. The enlightened among them consider themselves the born inheritors of other people's goods. The dull and stupid help themselves to what they can lay hands on in brutal silence. They can bring 17,000 soldiers into the field.

They are the North American Indians of Europe, possessing much the same hardihood and cunning, and the same love of torturing and mutilating their victims. What the scalp is to the Red Indian the nose is to the Montenegrin, and it matters not whether the foe be living or dead, the ghastly trophy is taken with equal delight. They differ, however, from the American savages in this, that they have had some training as soldiers, and they are armed with the weapons of more civilised warfare.

Russia's move was with Servia, and here she had a great advantage. The Serbs themselves are louts without much courage or capacity. Still they are far more numerous than the Montenegrins. Their country is rich in supplies for an army, and many of the fortresses are almost impregnable. She had no fighting faculty to speak of, but that could be imported.

Russia had another advantage in dealing with Servia. The Serb is easily managed. He is the most conceited creature alive. There is a story told in one of our books of adventure in the Polar regions, how a little Esquimaux, not four feet high, came on board of a whaling ship, and first of all took some food with the sailors; but seeing plenty of his own ordinary fare about he sat down, ate half-a-dozen pounds of whale blubber, drank a gallon of train oil, and then, rising in a state of supreme satisfaction with himself, rubbed his stomach and called himself *Kelite*, which means the lord of the whole creation.

The Serb, then, is, in his own estimation, *Kelite*, the supreme man in modern Europe, and is led by this stupid vanity wherever the cunning Russian likes to take him. Besides that, he happens just now to be governed by *professed politicians* and by a weak prince, who is nothing but a tool in their hands. It is a cruel game, but the Servian people are just now merely the cat's paw with which the Northern bear is stirring up the burning coals of a cruel war and are bearing all the consequences of contact with the fire.

CHAPTER VI.

SECRET SOCIETIES.

The Secret Societies of Europe form one of the most singular phenomena of our modern civilisation. They exist everywhere, and take their complexion in most instances from the RACE with which they originate. With the Celts—namely, the Irish branch of that family—the Secret Society is *Fenianism;* in France, Belgium, and other parts of the Continent it is the *International*. The special names given to the Russian Secret Societies are not always attainable. Some are *Nihilists,** others religious, but they are all Socialists, and abound throughout the Empire. The *Omladina* is composed of nearly the whole of the Slav population of Hungary, Poland and some other parts of Eastern Europe. The *Imperial*

---

* " A Nihilist," said Paul Petrovitch! "This word must come from the Latin *nihil* (nothing), and consequently it signifies a man who—who recognises nothing."

"Or rather, who respects nothing," said Paul Petrovitch, and buttered his bread.—" Fathers and Sons." (Translated from the Russian by Eugene Schuyler.)

Panslavonic organisation, whose head-quarters are at Moscow and its executive committee at Bucharest, and the pure Republican societies of Western Europe, of whom Garibaldi is the head, make up the principal political Secret Societies of Europe.

It is hardly necessary for the purpose for which this book is written to spend much time in defining either the principles or objects of those associations; they differ, of course, in different countries. Thus, the object of the Fenians is to drive the English out of Ireland and establish a Republic of Kilkenny Cats. The object of the Omladina in Hungary is somewhat similar: it is to crush the Magyar or dominant race and to convert Hungary into a province of the proposed Panslavonic Republic. The International, wherever it exists, is Communistic; and the Russian and Western branches differ in this—that the former would abolish the use of money altogether; they have, indeed, adopted More's Utopia as their ideal of what a State should be. The French, Swiss, and German branches found their ideal in the Commune established during the siege of Paris. They would use money and all the appliances of modern life; but would exterminate kings, priests, and capitalists. The Omladina desire to establish a Republic, as will be seen by our map, stretching from the Black Sea to the Adriatic and from the Adriatic to the Baltic; they would remove the capital of the Russ from St. Petersburg to Moscow, if not to Astrakan;

take the European provinces of Turkey as far as the Balkan, make Constantinople a Free City, and blot out Austria from the map of the world; reconstruct Poland, which, together with Bohemia and Hungary, would form free States in this great Republic.

There is one singular characteristic about all those societies whose objects we have defined; various as their purposes are, they all agree upon the means of obtaining their ends. It is war, murder, assassination, outrage, pillage. The Fenians, who tried to blow down the Clerkenwell House of Detention, attempted the assassination of the Duke of Edinburgh, and perpetrated the Manchester murders, are no better and no worse than their brother-rascals all the world over.

The influence those societies are exerting in the affairs of the world has been sketched by two able hands. In his speech at Aylesbury Lord Beaconsfield said—" Servia declared war upon Turkey—that is to say, the Secret Societies of Europe, through Servia, declared war upon Turkey. I can assure you, gentlemen, that in the attempt to conduct the government of this world there are new elements to be considered which our predecessors had not to deal with. We have not to deal only with Emperors, Princes, and Ministers, but there are the Secret Societies, an element which we must take into consideration, which, at the last moment, may baffle all your arrangements, which have their agents everywhere, which have reckless agents, which countenance assassination, and which, if necessary, could produce a massacre."

In the course of this work we shall have to give many instances of the manner in which those societies conduct their operations. It is enough here to name them and define their objects. In a despatch addressed to the Earl of Derby by Consul-General White, from Belgrade, April 28th, 1876, the following account is given of the Secret Societies which are at present influencing the attempt to break up the Turkish Empire:—

"In the political events which are either going on or preparing in this part of Europe two distinct Slav bodies are likely to exercise no small influence—viz., the Omladinists in Hungary and the Slavonic Committee in Moscow.

"The Omladinists are the Slav Home Rulers of Hungary; as such they are hated and despised by the governing (Magyar) class in that kingdom; and hitherto they had shown so defective a political organisation that their importance arose much more from their supposed connection with certain parties at Court at Vienna, and from their actual relations with the Revolutionary party in the Principality of Servia, than on account of any immediate influence as agitators in Croatia, Dalmatia, or Slavonia. Actual events are foreshowing a change in this respect.

"From 1849 to July 1875 these Slavs were chiefly aiming at the attainment of a recognition of certain Home Rule prerogatives by means of their opposition to Magyar or Hungarian supremacy. With that view they took up arms under Jellachitch for the Emperor Francis Joseph in 1849, opposed the restitution of the ancient Hungarian Constitution till 1867, and have carried on a more or less factious constitutional opposition to the dominant party since that year.

"But the sympathies which the Southern Slavs were able not only to set forth openly, but also to which they could give practical effect during six months, in favour of the insurgent Slavs in the Herzegovina, have modified their position, and the aspirations of that race have acquired fresh vigour from the Adriatic to the Drave, and from the Drave to the Theiss and the Save, by giving them a cohesion and a common bond of hope, by making them view the cause of the Turkish Rayahs as their own, and their emancipation from Ottoman rule as an object of primary importance for Austrian Slavs, by which they can attain an influence which they have not had for centuries, and which they have hitherto sought in vain on the hustings or in Parliamentary assemblies.

"Their proximity to the scene of the insurrection has enabled the Croats and Dalmatians to give the Insurgents far more real assistance than they can have derived from Servia, and the public men of the latter Principality have seen themselves gradually ousted by these, and by the Prince of Montenegro, from the leadership of the national cause, which Servia considered hitherto as its peculiar mission and attribute.

"The Sclavonic Committees in Russia, and especially the central one at Moscow, have contributed a good deal to propagate sympathy for the insurgent cause in the Russian Empire, and to collect funds for the support of that cause."*

It will thus be seen that the objects which those societies have in view can never be attained without the sacrifice of hundreds of thousands, and in some cases of millions of lives. To drive the English out of Ireland, the Magyars out of Hungary, and the Turks out of Europe means bloodshed on such a scale as the world has never yet seen.

The map of the past history of the world is traced in gore. Byron says, mournfully—

> "Let there be light, said God, and there was light;
> Let there be blood, said man, and there's a sea."

But this is not simply to be a sea, but an ocean; a Noahacian flood of the hearts' blood of the noblest portion of mankind; the wisest, bravest, best of men; the philosophers and men of science who teach; the ministers who stand before God's altar

---

* "Affairs of Turkey," No. III., p. 126.

and offer up great prayers for humanity; the noblest, purest, most beautiful, devout, and cultured women are all to be cast into the gehenna of fire, that the apostles of a "New Moral World" may inherit the earth.

CHAPTER VII.

RUSSIAN HOPES AND PURPOSES.

THE Empress of Russia is a politician and a Panslavist of the purest water. Never since "Catherine's reign, whom history still adores as greatest of all women"—never mind the rest—has any female sovereign exercised anything like the political influence displayed by the present Czarina. A quaint old philosopher lays it down as an axiom that man is undoubtedly the head of creation, but, he adds significantly, from his own experience, that woman is the neck, and generally turns it which way she pleases. In truth, His Imperial Majesty the Czar of all the Russias is henpecked. The reader must take this fact into account in looking at the singular and sometimes tortuous policy of Russia. The Empress has her own policy and her own pets. Kauffman, Ignatieff, and others, have her confidence and support. The Emperor gives his word of honour that a certain thing shall not be done; the Empress guarantees immunity for those who disobey the Imperial order. The Emperor sends the most solemn warnings to Servia and Montenegro not to make war against Turkey; the Empress sends Tchernaieff and the volunteers to declare and make war. It would be too much to say that his Imperial Majesty is under petticoat government, since the petticoat is not thrown over him at all. He is not like our late King William, who is caricatured peeping out of the pocket-hole of his wife's dress. They are past even the semblance of shame. His Imperial Majesty says what he likes and Her Imperial Majesty does what she pleases; hence the diplomatic despatches coming from the Emperor say one thing, the actions and policy of the Russian Government and people indicate something totally different.

As we before said, Her Majesty is a Panslavist, whole and entire, and is ready to use, not simply political influence, but to bring science, art, literature, and religion to aid the cause in which she has embarked. Here is an example of her method of working.

In May, 1867, an Ethnological Exhibition was got up in Moscow, the avowed object of which was the prosecution of anthropological studies. This, however, was only the pretence; its real purpose was to have Panslavonic meetings, in which the dismemberment of the Turkish Empire could be discussed, and the best method of disposing of Austria be determined upon.

The distinguished *savans* who assembled to dispose of so much of the world that did not belong to them, had the honour of being presented to their Majesties the Emperor and Empress of Russia. On this occasion Her Majesty displayed her talent in a remarkable manner. The *Times* newspaper report says:—

" Her Majesty deigned to express her regret that the various Slavonian races had not a common alphabet and orthography. This feeling was taken up warmly by some Servians and Czechs present and bore immediate fruit. No sooner had the travellers reached Moscow, and with their Russian friends formed themselves into a Slavonic Congress, than improving upon Her Majesty's sentiment, they determined that the Slavonic tribes to achieve unity must select one of their several languages to be the common literary language of all, and that the idiom so honoured could be only Russian. The *Slovansky Svet*, a Czechian paper subsequently established at Prague to pave the way to this end, thus dilated upon this resolve :—

"'To the Slavonic Congress at Moscow it was given to advance the cause of Slavonian solidarity very considerably. To this memorable Panslavonic meeting we are indebted for the conversion of Slavonic solidarity from sounding phrase to living reality. The sharers in this Slavonic pilgrimage to Russia, the most eminent men from the Slavonic races, have declared it to be imperatively necessary that the Russian language be made the common and exclusive literary language of all Slavonic races. This announcement has been unanimously approved by the whole Slavonian Press.'"

We have put Her Majesty first, the grey mare being the better horse, but the language of the mighty Czar to the interesting foreigners was still more decided:—

"We have always looked upon the Servians as our brothers, and I hope that God will permit your affairs to take a more favourable turn at no distant future. God grant that all your wishes may be speedily fulfilled. . . . I salute you, my dear Slavonian brethren, on this our common Slavonian soil."

Prince Gortchakoff uses even more pointed expressions than his master, and evidently had an eye to the events which have just taken place in Eastern Europe. He says, with a supreme ignorance or disregard of ethnological truths:—

"The Servians are a youthful nation, and one having a destiny to fulfil. I am old, and perhaps shall not live to see the day when my prophecy shall be borne out by fact; but depend upon it, my successors will have the interests of the Servian people as much at heart as I have."

The sentiments of those in the higher circles of Russian life were faithfully re-echoed by those immediately below them. At a dinner given in honour of Count Tolstoy, the Minister of Education, and M. Pogseboff, Mayor of St. Petersburg, M. Bolit, a Croatian demagogue, said:—

"The battle of Sadowa has decided the destinies of the European East. In consequence of it the German world has been separated from the Slavonian. What remains to be done is to solve the Slavonian question—a task to be fulfilled by the Slavonians themselves, and chiefly by Russia. Russia, gentleman, is no longer Russian; it is Slavonian—nay, Panslavonian. The resources at her disposal are not only material, but also moral. Slavonic Russia is no menace to civilisation, but only prepares Europe for witnessing the re-union of the Slavonian family. The first blow in the great struggle must be the cutting through the Eastern knot. This is a matter affecting as much the honour of the Russian people as the interests of the Russian Empire. We, the Eastern Slavonians—we, the Eastern orthodox Christians—we, the Servians, hope and trust that Russia will not forget the catastrophe of Kossof, which overthrew the Servian Empire, but soon do her duty and commence her appointed work. I propose the speedy solution of the Eastern Question."

This means that now, when Austria has been

separated from and is no longer protected by Germany, there is nothing to prevent the Slavonians from utilising her for those Panslavonic purposes, to be carried out under Russian auspices. But before Austria can be effectually taken in hand, Turkey must be swept from the scene. The Croat's greeting was reciprocated by a Russian poet, M. Markevitch, reciting a hymn whose tone and purport a single strophe will suffice to display:—

"Although torn asunder by envious fate, the Slavs have never ceased to be one nation, the sons of one mother. It is this which the world cannot pardon in us; yet you will never desert Russia, nor will Russia desert you. The world is frightened at all Slavonians standing together, and addressing the nations as one. Having long subjected us to injury and insult, and knowing well that the remembrance of our sufferings will never be effaced from our hearts, the world is scared by the Slavonian revival, and dreads the judgment of God."

Similar statements were vented by Count Tolstoy, the Slavophil member of the Russian Cabinet, who spoke of the grand future in store for the great Slavonian race, and somewhat guardedly observed:—

"Real feeling is never manifested so much in words as in the flash of the eye, and in the features of the human countenance divine. . . . . Were you to roam from one end to the other of the vast Empire, on which the sun never sets, you would carry with you the sympathies of the 70,000,000 of the Czar's subjects."

All those suggestions about Panslavism point to one distinct place, the conquest of Constantinople. The Imperial Panslavists would make it the capital of their empire; the Republican branch desires to convert it into a free city, with the Bosphorus open to the ships of all nations. There is a little difficulty in getting there, though it is remarkable with what ease the Slavs dispose of it.

Shortly after the anthropological meetings just referred to, General Fadéeff published a pamphlet in St. Petersburg, "with the permission of the censorship." We may observe that the General was, at the time, a candidate for the post of Minister of War. He is described as a burning and shining light of the Panslavists, and what he says, therefore, may be regarded as the thoughts and aspirations of that party.

The General almost entirely ignores the Turks as a military power, although they were the conquerors at Oltanitza and Khalifat; have held their own during the present generation at least, and have just* cut the Servio-Russian army to pieces. The General is also equally certain that France and England "are not in a position to defend European Turkey against Russia, provided the hands of Russia are united on the western frontier. It is a matter of

---

* November 1st, 1876.

impossibility to struggle by landing forces against a Power of equal strength which has open access overland into the disputed country. . . . The Russian army requires only six weeks, and even less, to march from the Danube to Constantinople, provided, of course, it be sufficiently numerous for the blockade of fortresses in the rear. . . . In order to settle the fate of European Turkey in spite of the maritime Powers, it will be sufficient for 150,000 troops to reach the Bosphorus—*i.e*, that 250,000 on the broadest calculation should reach the Danube. . . . Russia can always forestall the land forces of her Western opponents, not only in the Balkans but even at Constantinople. Even if they should succeed after considerable difficulty in meeting the Russian army in front of that capital with a force like that which, after the lapse of many months, they got together in 1854, at Varna, 60,000 Europeans, supported by any number of Turks, would not be able to defeat a Russian army of 150,000 men. . . . The Straits would fall into the hands of the captors of Constantinople; their fortifications could not hold out against a land force; and, the entrances to the Sea of Marmora once occupied and properly defended, any serious attempt from seaward to dispute the possession of Turkey would become impossible."

This cheerful view, however, is sicklied o'er by the pale cast of incertitude; for, says General Fadéef—

"The difficulty is this, that it is impossible for Russia to carry on a war on the Balkan peninsula without the permission of Austria, and that permission she can under no circumstances obtain."

For the key of the gate formed by the south-east angle of the Danube and the Carpathians is held by Austria, and without her passport the Lower Danube is inaccessible. In a word, Russia's experience is that to her Turkey is like a strong chest of which Austria is the lid. "Without lifting that lid," says the General, "it is impossible to get anything out of the chest." Can the bottom of the chest be knocked out by a landing from the Bosphorus?

No, replies the General; "the seizure of Constantinople and the Straits would not settle the question. It would have to be settled by a war on land against a coalition of which Austria would be the soul. . . . In order to occupy the Straits and the entire peninsula, it would be necessary to detach forces greater than those which would be required in the case of a war with the West to defend the shores and land frontier of Russia against a live Turkey. . . . The naval Powers alone could not bar the road to the Bosphorus against Russia, even by force of arms; Austria can arrest Russia without firing a gun merely by her armed neutrality. Nay, more, she can further protect the Turk by opening a road to the Vistula by revolutionising Poland, as she threatened to do in 1856."

Need we say that, entertaining, as he does, those views, our author holds that for Austria

"It would be an act of suicide on her part to consent to a solution of the Eastern Question in a Russian sense, or even in a sense that might not be diametrically opposed to Russian views and feelings. The existence of free Slavonian States side by side with extensive Slavonian provinces in a state of thraldom—provinces with inhabitants that are not only of the same blood, but that also form one people speaking the same tongue on both sides of the Save—is quite incompatible. On one bank of a rivulet, across which a fowl might wade, would be free Skuptchinas and a happy future, on the other a gradual disappearance of a national identity which had hitherto existed in the form of an inferior race, without the slightest prospects, and which would not become either German or Magyar. Is such a state of things possible? Austria lost her Italian possessions because she admitted next door the existence of a small independent Italian kingdom. How can she be expected to consent to the creation along her southern boundary of a Slavonian Piedmont, which, from its national homogeneity, would carry dissolution not only into one corner of her possessions, but into the very body of the Empire?

General Fadéeff frankly admits that Austria

and Turkey must stand or fall together. He says:—

"Austria can hold her part of the Slavonian mass as long as Turkey holds hers, and *vice versâ*. This position of affairs determines the relations of Austria towards the Eastern Question, apart even from the will of her statesmen. . . . It would appear, therefore, that of the historical question—*i.e.*, the question of the weakness of Turkey, the name alone remains. . . . Another question still more important, and which can only be called the Panslavist question, has grown from under it. . . . A Slavonian family question, depicted on the map in two different colours, but indivisible in reality, and not to be solved except conjointly; for the reciprocal connection of both parts of the question is now an undoubted fact, and one that cannot be affected by any eventualities. . . . Europe purposely averts her eyes from a dangerous unity, and does not wish to see it. Russia cannot however but see it. She stands with her face to the West, and the rising sun does not dazzle her eyes."

He recognises the danger to Russia of her present position. She has conquered too much or too little. He adds:—

"The historical move of Russia from the Dnieper to the Vistula was a declaration of war to Europe, which have broken into a part of the Continent that did not belong to her. Russia now stands in the midst of the enemy's lines. Such a condition is only temporary: she must either drive back the enemy or abandon her position."

In this way we are to see the Czar of Russia reigning over the liberated soil of Eastern Europe, "long recognised, in the expectation of the people as the direct heir of Constantine the Great." The spirit of the age, it would appear, admits of but two solutions of the Eastern Question, " either Russia as a local Empire of the Russian race, or Russia as a concentration of the Slav and Orthodox world." Therefore her policy must, says General Fadéeff, be " to wait and to act." She must engender the intellectual and moral impulses and yearnings of Panslavism on both sides of the line that divides her from "the last enslaved remnants of the Russian race." For this, we are told, " there will be no lack of favourable opportunities; the nineteenth century is not an age of peace or tranquil prosperity in Europe." Even if it were, General Fadéef warns us that, " however great that unanimity, and however favourable the opportunity, this great question can only be settled by force, and first by Russian might alone." This is the Russian dream of an iron Panslavonic Empire.

It is a singular circumstance in the history of this great Panslavic movement that no one can even surmise, much less determine, with whom it originated. Two or three people, to whom it evidently does not belong, claim the honour of first conceiving the grand idea. The most probable account is that it was the work of a Polish spy in the pay of Russia, who, having nothing else to report to his employers, sent a scheme for the embodying the whole of Europe wherever any Slavs existed into one great nationality.

The idea was laid hold of by two directly opposite parties.* The Poles were in despair of ever re-establishing their kingdom. The massacre of the nobles by the peasants; the brutal manner in which their insurrections had been put down by Russia, aided by Germany and Austria, had drowned in patriotic blood the idea, but not the hope, of the restoration of their nationality. They caught, therefore, the spy's suggestion as the sheet-anchor of their salvation; it was broad, grand, and afforded a field for the ambition of a numerous race scattered in several kingdoms. It opened, also, a new propaganda. Up to that time the Poles had been trying, through diplomatic and international intervention, to restore the Polish monarchy. In Panslavism they found a wider field for the exercise of their talents; and they had also a discontented population in Russia, Turkey, Austria, and Germany to work upon. The result was that the existing secret organisations were

---

* The Secret Society, called the "United Sclavonians," founded about 1820, proclaimed that all Sclavonians were brothers, and that the interests of the Pole and the Russian were the same. (Frost, "Secret Societies," II., 95). It was a Russian Society, formed by a number of young officers who had served in the Army of Occupation of France" (*ib*. II. 96.).

greatly extended: Panslavism became the watchword and the Panslavic Republic, as shown in our map, the hope of the Slavs. It will be seen by a glance at that drawing that the proposed Republic extended from the Dnieper almost to St. Petersburg, which was to be a free city, along the coast of the Black Sea to the Balkan range, across from there to the Adriatic, from the Adriatic to the Baltic, making the Oder the boundary line of the Republic toward Germany. Various circumstances have, however, greatly modified this bold scheme. The crushing of the Russian power during the Crimean War may be said to have converted Russia to Panslavism; and the consolidation of the German Empire has forced upon Russian and all Panslavonic statesmen the formidable fact that the lion in their path is United Germany. Lord Derby asked the other day, or rather suggested, that the important question in relation to Turkey was, Who should occupy Constantinople? To Germany there is a prior question—Who shall command the Danube and hold Trieste; and involved in that is the great struggle for predominance in Central Europe? Can Germany give up her Polish provinces at the dictation of the Panslavists, and can she afford to have a mighty Republic or Empire for her neighbour which breathes nothing but deadly hatred to the German race?

Pushkin, a Russian poet, writing in 1831, when

Panslavism was young, propounds this important question. He says:—

"Shall the Slavonic streams be united in the Russian Sea, or the latter be dried up?"*

It was not until 1854 that this question was very definitely answered in the affirmative on Russia's part. The Crimean War had so broken the military power of the old Russian party, that something new, fresh, tangible, and hopeful, was required.

That hope, if Russia had her military power alone to depend on, was now broken; but if she could move the whole Slavic population of the world, foment rebellions in Turkey, Austria, and Germany, and intervene in "the cause of humanity" whenever the opportunity occurred for extending her

---

* I am indebted to the Rev. Ponsonby Lyons for the following translation of this poem:—

"To the Calumniators of Russia.

"Why do you make a noise, popular orators, in confusing infatuation? Why do you curse and threaten the holy Russian land? What has so stirred you up?—Poland's insurrection? Be silent. Your understanding solves not this question. It is an old strife in the Slavic race, and the look of no stranger can here decide the right. Most ancient and manifold are the sufferings already begotten by the quarrel. Often already has one people, of the two, bowed before the storm of the thunder and lightning. Who will appear as victor in the unequal strife? Does the balance incline to the Pole, the false, or to the true Russian? Will the Slavic rivers unite themselves in the Russian sea? Will it dry up? that is the weighty question."—(From "Bodenstedt's Translation of Alexander Pushkin's Poetical Works," I., 25.)

empire, then the case was not desperate. Hence the Panslavonic Republic was annexed to the domain of Holy Russia.

The map was impudent enough. The statistical table which accompanied it was, if possible, more audacious and misleading. We give it here for what it is worth, which is not much.

It is based on the susposition that there are more than 78,000,000 Slavs in the world, which, thank God, is not true. It also assumes that those Slavs are strong, and will soon be a dominant race, which we are doubly thankful to know is neither a fact in the present nor a possibility in the future.

SURVEY OF THE SLAVONIC POPULATIONS,

According to the Different States to which they belong.

(Computed by Szafiarik in 1842.)

	Russia.	Austria.	Prussia.	Turkey.	Republic of Cracow.	Saxony.	Total.
Great Russians, or Muscovites	35,314,000	...	...	...	...	...	35,314,000
Little Russians, or Malorusses	10,370,000	2,774,000	...	...	...	...	13,144,000
White Russians	2,726,000	...	...	...	...	...	2,726,000
Bulgarians	80,000	7,000	...	3,500,000	...	...	3,587,000
Servians, or Illyrians	100,000	2,594,000	...	2,600,000	...	...	5,294,000
Croates	...	801,000	...	...	...	...	801,000
Carynthians	...	1,151,000	...	...	...	...	1,151,000
Poles	4,912,000	2,341,000	1,982,000	...	130,000	...	9,365,000
Bohemians and Moravians	...	4,370,000	44,000	...	...	...	4,414,000
Slovaks in Northern Hungary	...	2,753,000	...	...	...	...	2,753,000
Lusatians and Vends { Upper	...	...	38,000	...	...	60,000	98,000
Lusatians and Vends { Lower	...	...	44,000	...	...	...	44,000
Total	53,502,000	16,791,000	2,108,000	6,100,000	130,000	60,000	78,691,000

CHAPTER VIII.

THE TURK AND THE SLAV.

ABOUT half a century ago, Pritchard, Lawrence, and others, who justly take rank among the first men of genius, and to whose careful labours and discoveries we owe the noble science of Ethnology, made known to the world the fact that a new race had, within a few centuries past, made its appearance in the great family of Mankind. The precise time and circumstances of its birth could not be exactly traced, but the broad fact remained that a branch of the great Mongolian variety of man had given birth to a people of the Caucasian type. That they owed their origin to a Mongul source was evident from the fact that they spoke a language, a branch of the Turanian, which is understood by people of that class, who are scattered from the frontiers of China to the frozen ocean in European Russia, and from Siberia to India.

But they were not Monguls, nor Tartars; they were a distinct race and people to themselves—the

Osmanli.* It was the opening of a new fountain of the life's blood of humanity. Various theories were suggested to account for this phenomena, such a mixture of blood by intermarriage with the Circassians and Mingrilians; this, however, would in no way account for the great facts of their physical and intellectual structure, and those who, like Vambery, have gone to seek for their ancestors in Central Asia, have not found them, for the simple reason there are none there. The Turk came out of that bleak region as Israel came out of Egypt, descended upon the fertile plains of Asia Minor and Eastern Europe, and there founded a mighty Empire: an Empire that is in its boyhood at present, or rather let us say emerging from it, half man and half boy, with the daring flush of youth on his face, a torrent of rich vermillion blood rushing through his arteries, and his nerves vibrating with celestial fires. But his fez is greasy, his tunic seedy, and the cuffs travelling fast towards the elbows; his baggy trousers are too short for him, and his toes are peeping through his shoes. But as the Americans say, he has "true grit" in him, and the schoolmaster, barber, tailor and shoemaker, will in no long time give him a proper outfit, both in brain and body.

But the Turk made a much greater conquest than

---

* See Pritchard's "Natural History of Man," paragraphs "Turks," pp. 209-214. See also Latham, Gliddon, Morton, and Knox, on the same subject.

that of the rich plains of Asia Minor and Eastern Europe. He stretched out his hand, grasped the sword of Allah and Islam, and the whole Mussulman world recognised in him its rightful holder. It was, as has often been the case in a severely contested battle-field, when some soldier of daring, genius and heroic courage steps to the front, and the whole army, by one electric impulse, follows in the path of victory and glory. The Moslems had always had enemies, Pagan as well as Christian, and they recognised in this young giant the champion of their faith.

He was welcomed to this position on the pure principle of " natural selection." He was the strongest. The quality, size, and distribution of his brain; his deep chest and healthy digestion; his faith in the All-Father, his contempt of danger and fearlessness of death, made him the rightful bearer of "the banner of the faithful." And the faithful are neither few nor feeble, as the Slavs will find before this great conflict is over.

The Turk, then, is the Englishman of the East; is of the same variety of mankind; a similar structure of brain; has the same indomitable courage; the same love of truth and contempt for lies and liars. And, singularly enough, our destinies are involved in the same fate. A free Turkey, by which we mean freedom from the constant intermeddling of foreign powers as well as a free people, left to her natural growth, secures and extends our influence in the East. But when Turkey falls our Oriental sun will go down beyond a sea of blood. It is the belief of my soul, that as the Lord of truth and righteousness liveth and reigneth, neither of these events will happen.

For the Turk is young, and England also is hardly yet in the full flush of her manhood, and we may therefore contrast their fresh young blood with the ancient and puddle life-stream of the Slavs.

And here it may be as well to remark, once for all, that the governing class in Russia are not Slavs at all; that the pure Russ is not a Slav; and even if he were it would not change the matter much, since the Government of Russia is to such an extent in the hands of Germans that SEVENTY-FIVE PER CENT. OF THE HIGHER CLASS of officials are Teutons. They are hated bitterly by the Slavs, hence the spread of Secret Societies, and if an army of the Emperor should ever fall into another Sedan beyond the Danube a Commune would very soon be declared in Moscow.

The Slav is almost the greatest failure nature ever made in her attempts to create a civilised man. Heaven only knows when the race first made its appearance on the face of the earth, since it was before the date of authentic history. When Prince Gortchakoff, therefore, talks of the Serbs being "a young and promising nation," destined to future

E

greatness, he is speaking to and of a race that was old and loutish two thousand years ago. "They have always been that which their names imply—a servile, slavish people, destined to fill up hidden corners of geography, and to become the tools of ambition. Heraclius used them as Gortchakoff does now; the Goths and Huns exploited or expelled them; from the Cæsars to Charlemagne they never once founded a nation; they feebly lent themselves to Attila at Rome and Chalons, as they lend themselves now to Tchernaieff; and their unmanly behaviour in the present war, while it emphasises the cruelty of forcing such poor swineherds to fight, reproduces every trait of the ancient stock as described by Procopius. Russian diplomacy talks exquisite French, and the Russian Court and nobility are splendid; but the country itself is little less barbarian than it was when the Sarmatians were combated by Marcus Aurelius. Not three per cent. of the Muscovite peasants can read and write. Their religion is an idolatrous superstition; their Government is a theocratic despotism; their wars are ferocious; their peace is a dreary servility. If, therefore, it be true that the Asiatic and Slavonic elements of the Russian Empire are really animated by a common impulse for conquest, what is coming for Europe is such a spectacle as when in the time of Valens, the Alans and Ostrogoths came down—'a tempest of tribes,' as Jornandes called them—on Adrianople, and classical civilisation began to perish."—*Daily Telegraph*.

No contrast can be greater than the conduct of the Slav when compared with the Turk during the present Servian war. On one side there was bravery and patient endurance of wrong, and it was only when the terrible excitement occurred in Bulgaria that the Mussulmans ever lost their coolness and self-possession. The Slav was a sneak, a coward, and an assassin from the first; he had no mercy even upon those of his own faith. The insurrection—as it is called in Herzegovina—was commenced by burning down the Christian villages, sending the women, children, and aged people into Bosnia or the Austrian territories; robbing and murdering the Moslems, and pressing the young men into their ranks to serve as soldiers. All the telegrams from them that appeared in the English papers about battles that had been fought and victories won, are purely fictitious. The first time the insurgents ever met the Sultan's troops was so late as May 23rd, 1876. Writing from Moslar on May 25th, 1876, Consul Holmes says:—"On the 23rd a large band of insurgents attacked a body of troops engaged in cutting wood at Tchernitza, in Gatzko. Reinforcements were sent to their assistance, and in the evening the soldiers returned to their quarters victorious. The affair is not important, but it may be remarked that this is, perhaps, the first instance of the rebels attacking the troops without the inducement of any convoy or pillage."

Personally the Slav is dull, sluggish, possessed of inordinate self-conceit and an apathy for all suffering which does not touch his own nervous organisation. He evidently thinks, with Falstaff, that "discretion is the better part of valour," and hence will never meet the Turk in open fight if the numbers be anything like equal, or if there be any possibility of running away. He even adopts the lowest form of cowardice—self-mutilation.*

Dr. MacCormac has just returned from the seat

---

* Their most able and zealous advocate, Mr. Meghan, of the *Daily News*, gives the following example of Bulgarian *manhood* (?):— "We were passing some bullock waggons one day that were driven by peasants, and although the latter had given us the road, my Mohammedan driver, through carelessness, allowed his wheel to strike the wheel of one of the waggons. Hereupon he instantly began to swear at the Bulgarian bullock driver so fiercely that, although he was unarmed, the other dropped everything and fled across the fields like a deer, leaving his little boy in the waggon. He was a tall, strong man, of forty perhaps, and it was pitiful to see a man so terror-stricken, and with so little manhood left in him; and more pitiful still to see the little boy abandoned, alone in the waggon, likewise terror-stricken, and crying after his father. My driver laughed and drove on, and everybody in my party seemed to regard the occurrence as the most natural thing in the world. These people, it would seem, grow up in fear and trembling from their cradles." Mr. Meghan seems to forget that this caitiff is what his ancestors were, and have been in all their generations, and yet we are asked to make an "autonomous" Eastern Europe for the like of him to govern.

of war, and an interesting paper in the *Lancet* gives an account of his medical experiences:—

"The kind of injuries met with among the Turks was, however, very different from those seen in the Servian hospitals. The number of Servian soldiers wounded in the left hand was very great, Mr. MacCormac, on the road from Belgrade to Alexinatz, having counted in seven or eight hours 100 men who had been wounded in the left hand. There were, on the other hand, no self-mutilators among the Turkish soldiers, who are described as being of fine physique; while the Servian stragglers met with on the road to Alexinatz were mere peasants, who would do anything rather than fight, and shot themselves, and sometimes also their officers, rather than go to battle."

Speaking of the brutal apathy of the Servian people, it adds:—

"The want of sympathy shown by most of the Servian peasantry was almost incredible. At Brazan Mr. MacCormac found two men lying on the roadside. One was wounded in the leg, and evidently had walked as far as he was able; the limb was swollen and inflamed, and the poor man was suffering agony. The other was cold, half collapsed, and smeared over with his own excrement, in the midst of which he was lying. Yet the villagers looked idly on, and did not attempt to relieve in any way the sufferings and distress of their fellow creatures, although there was an empty house close by, with stretchers in it, where the poor men might have lain in comparative comfort, sheltered from the broiling sun. Mr. MacCormac likens the apathy of these ignorant peasants to the conduct of wild beasts, who drive their sick and wounded companions out of the herd."

The Rev. Frank L. Hopkins, having spent four months in Servia for the purpose of studying the people during the present war, who is a Liberal in politics, and went out inspired by the deep sympathy which he had with the Servian people, in a lecture giving some account of his adventures, said:—

"The Servian people had rendered themselves conspicuous for ingratitude to their best rulers, even to the extent of assassination. They had been notorious for baseness, for treachery, for cowardice, yet for a vain parade of bravery. In the present war, when they had proclaimed that they had fought a battle and obtained a victory, he had been on a neighbouring height, and had seen nothing which could be called a battle, and instead of a victory the Servian troops had retreated *sauve qui peut;* thousands of them not once, and others but once, having discharged their rifles. The treatment of their wounded had been characterised by the most culpable disregard and negligence, while the Turks in their comfortable hospitals made provisions equal to that of the best English infirmaries. In Servia he never slept without having his revolver at hand; whereas in the houses of the Turks he needed no such precaution. Many of the alleged 'horrible atrocities' were inventions. He had certain knowledge that the foundation for the story that the Turks roasted the prisoners alive was no other than that the Servians themselves picked up some of their slain from the field, fastened them to trees, and put fire under them, for the purpose of appealing to what they hoped would be a world-wide sympathy. Some of the more reckless agents of the press from England had favoured and promulgated the calumny, knowing that it was a gross deception."

If it were necessary we could continue to give testimonies of this kind through scores of pages. The remarkable thing about the whole is that in the hundreds of pages that I have been obliged to wade through in preparing this book there is not one good or generous deed recorded of the Serb.

It will be remembered that this outbreak was forced upon the Turk without cause and without warning, and our consuls in different parts of the disturbed districts have sent their reports to Lord Derby, and they all, with one single exception, bear the highest testimony to the patient forbearance and calmness under the greatest outrages and of their bravery whenever called upon to face an enemy.

Consul Holmes, writing from Bosnia-Seraï, June

15, 1876, describes the condition of the Mussulmans there as trying in the extreme. They knew that the Panslavists had doomed them to utter destruction, and, in conversation with him, many of them admitted that their position was almost unbearable. The threat, which they knew from the experience of their brethren in Herzegovina was not an idle one, that they were the marked victims to the Moloch of Panslavism, their homes to be the fire through which the whole family, to the babe upon the breast, were to pass, made inaction nearly beyond human endurance. They were brave, armed, and in such a case would meet a martyr's death according to their faith. They heard every day how the Moslems were treated in the districts around them, and although there was some wild exaggeration in those reports, still there was a substantial basis of truth in them, which showed that the massacre of the Turks in Europe had begun, and that those who commenced would, if they had the power, carry it to the bitter end—the destruction of over four million and a half of people. A deluge of blood, which would make all others small in comparison to it.

And yet they remained calm, orderly, and neighbourly with their Christian fellow-subjects. Consul Holmes says:—" I think that the conduct of the Mussulman population in the interior of Bosnia has hitherto been most praiseworthy, but they are becoming wearied and exasperated by seeing matters going from bad to worse." And they did go on to worse. Servia not only declared war, but her cutthroat emissaries made their way into Bosnia and perpetrated many outrages upon the Moslems there. Still, there has been no outbreak of Mahometan fanaticism, nor have the Moslems committed any outrage in that principality.

If the reader will refer again to the utterance of Prince Gortchakoff, it will be observed that Albania was one of the districts in which troubles might be anticipated, or perhaps we, who are under no necessity for using diplomatic language, may say had been planned. The Panslavist agitators had been there with money and arms, and had, as is their evil fashion, incited the Christians to murder their Moslem neighbours.

Consul Kirby Green, in a despatch to Lord Derby, dated Scutari, July 24, 1876, says:—

"Although a good deal is heard of the atrocities of the Mohammedans against the Christians in other parts of the Empire, here, in North Albania, where Moslems are daily being shot down by the Montenegrins and by rebel Slav tribes, the Turkish troops, both regular and irregular, have not committed a single act which could be called an outrage. Many of the peasantry near Podgoritza are known to sympathise with the Montenegrins, but still their crops are standing and they carry on their agricultural labours unmolested on each side of the military high roads. I myself, as a European, have met with more than courtesy from all ranks in the Turkish army, and the only feeling I have been able to observe is one of resignation at having to carry out a war which has been forced upon them."

Such is the contrast between the two races which are brought into conflict on this great Eastern Question.

CHAPTER IX.

ISLAM.

But the Turk is the champion of Islam, and, before proceeding, let us pause here for a moment and glance at that form of faith in God, Humanity and Eternal Life.

Among the great and most potent forms of religion that the world has ever seen is that of Mohammedanism. Originating as it did in a country always considered sterile and contemptible, and at a period in the history of that country the most dark and despairing it had ever witnessed, this new form of faith produced changes little short of miraculous. Most of the men who had any pretensions to learning were Atheists;* the generality, gross and grovelling idolators; they were almost bandits by profession, and had descended to that point of

---

* "Some of the Pagan Arabs believed neither a creation past nor a resurrection to come, attributing the origin of things to nature, and their dissolution to age."—Sale's " Introduction to the Koran," p. 21.

immorality in which, for want of truth and virtue, social life had become well nigh impossible.

As the chemist standing over his retorts, in which guano, coal tar, or other fœtid and poisonous elements are all seething, transforms the mass into the most useful substances, and colours that will rival the Tyrian dye, so Mahomet from this mass of scepticism, depravity, and helplessness, evolved out of it a nation, or brotherhood of humanity, whose heroism will contrast favourably with the most celebrated characters or nations in history.

In speaking thus of ISLAM, I wish it to be distinctly understood that I am a Christian; that I think, speak, feel, believe, hope to live, die, and be for ever a Christian—nay, more, I believe in an ever-living Christ—in His Presence among us, perpetual and everlasting. To me the Word is made flesh, and dwells among us, and whatsoever is done to the least of the little ones who come fresh from the All Father is done unto Him. Are little innocents burnt on brigand bayonets, then is Christ cast into the fire; are they starved, then do His lips lack bread; are they homeless, then the Son of Man hath not where to lay His head; are they ill-treated, then is the Saviour scourged; and if they are put to death, then is He crucified afresh and put to open shame.

I may add, further, that next to the Captain of our Salvation my ideal of a Christian man is John, not the Baptist, but the Evangelist. Peter, Paul, and all the other Apostles are, in my estimation, far below the "disciple whom Jesus loved;" who stood by the Cross on Calvary when all the rest had fled, who took the greatest and most exalted of women as his mother and was unto her a son. Even in intellectual grasp I regard him as being far above Paul. The latter had learning, culture, logic, discipline, and ambition. John was absorbed in love and full of the Divine Light. His Gospel is *the* Gospel, for it is full of the Saviour's heart; his epistles are the outcome of the deepest affection; and it was given to him, and to him alone, to witness the unfolding of the great blazon of the future. I am so thoroughly *en rapport* with John that I almost fancy myself now standing with him on Patmos' barren isle, and watching the "pale horse" with its rider Death emerging from the north.* After John my love and admiration of inspiration and genius becomes general: Shakespere, the poet of humanity; Swedenborg, its seer; and, as the Koran says, "the companions of the companions of God in all ages."

I am disposed to give the "unlettered prophet of Arabia" a high place in the Valhalla of those who have been termed the "first-born sons of light."

---

* "And I looked, and behold a pale horse; and his name that sat upon it was Death, and Hell followed with him. And power was given to him over the fourth part of the earth to kill with sword and hunger."—Rev. vi., 8.

Since Mahomet slept no other has arisen to exercise any such potent influence on mankind. We have had Reformers, and great and noble ones, but no such creators of new nations as he was.

My ideal man in the Christian sphere is John. Among the prophet heroes of Israel it is Elijah. The latter was Mahomet's model. He could not stand on Patmos like John, and accept martyrdom as the seal of his mission; but he could call all the world to assemble on Carmel, as Elijah did, throw the sword into the scale, and take the consequence of the turn of the beam, fully believing that the balances were in the hand of God, and that whatever HE did was right.

In thinking of the man in this form, we must also take into account the circumstances by which he was surrounded. It was a life and death struggle in the most absolute sense of the words. From the first announcement of his mission, he was doomed to death by the majority of the community in which he lived—a majority of about eighteen out of every twenty persons composing it. After confounding his enemies by his superior intelligence he was obliged to seek safety in flight; he was pursued, and delivered from his foes by what appeared to him a miracle. But their thirst for his blood was not slaked by his absence. He had fled, as Elijah did from Ahab, and when safety was no longer possible in flight, he came back, as the Prophet did to the field of Naboth, and dared his enemies to an ordeal of which God should be the umpire. From henceforth his mission was clear and decided; his enemies fought with the coward's sword of falsehood. His was the sword of Allah and of Islam, tempered in the waters of Divine truth. He conquered, and his success from this time was never doubtful.

Taken as a man of genius, I reckon Mahomet among the very highest. He was unlettered; never to the end of his life could decipher the alphabet of his own language. And yet he dictated a book, which has ever since, and ever will, take its rank among the Bibles of the world. We miss in him the polished phrases and high culture of Isaiah, and the logic of Paul, but there is a force, a grandeur, and a universality, accompanied by a definiteness of purpose, which can hardly be met with elsewhere. Neither had he any military education or training, and yet he founded an organised army, which broke in pieces the trained and disciplined forces of the world. Still he was not a warrior but a propagandist; he fully believed that the good people of this world ought to govern it. That it was their mission, to which God had appointed them. Equally deep was his conviction that the unbelievers, whose misfortune it was to believe in lies, and follow the father of them, should be governed by the lovers of truth and the doers of righteousness. Hence his conditions of warfare: "Lay down your arms, embrace the true faith, and be brothers. Retain your own faith, but pay us a reasonable tribute for governing you righteously and in the name of Allah; or, take the sword and fight, and let God decide between us."

It will thus be seen that Mahomet was not in the ordinary sense of the word a conqueror; his mission as he conceived it, was to bring the kingdoms of this world into subjection to the will of Allah, and whatever errors there might be in this grand conception, or mistakes in executing his design, the means he adopted were perfectly in accordance with the highest genius, and his own prophetic mission.

He did not live to carry out his design of invading Syria, but his generals who acted on his instructions took an army into the field, the like of which the world had never hitherto seen.

There was not A DRUNKARD, A GAMBLER, A LIAR, OR A COWARD in the whole host.

The historians who have given an account of the going forth of this army have left a record of how the worthless elements were eliminated from it. When the invasion of Syria was first determined on, and a host collected, the magnitude and the hazard of the undertaking was laid before the whole army, and every man among them was exhorted to return home if he had any fear in his heart. If he did not love truth and eternal life before all earthly considerations, and if he did not offer himself a living sacrifice, in which life and death were matters of equal indifference, he was to turn back. Many did return, only to repent of their cowardice, and rejoin the army of invasion. Again: When Abu Obeidah was prosecuting his invasion of Syria, he found that some of his men had fallen into the habit of drinking wine, and taking plunder on their own account. They were not numerous, but the army had to be purged of such disorderly comrades. A proclamation was issued, not only condemning such proceedings, and ordering those who were known as guilty to be punished, but exhorted all who had been guilty of those sins in secret to come forward and confess their guilt and receive the punishment, which, according to the sentence of Ali the Prophet's son-in-law, was four score blows upon the soles of their feet. They came to a man, and drinking and stealing were thus banished from the army.*

---

* One brave old toper took his punishment, and, as an American would say, "liquored up" on the strength of it. His example, it was feared, would be infectious; and though he was one of the bravest of the Moslems, Abu Midjan was put in irons, and from the house-top was an impotent witness of the battle of Cadesia, where the Mussulmans were sustaining a grievous defeat. He implored the general Saad's wife to set him free, and supply him with a horse and arms, swearing by all that was esteemed holy to return and resume his fetters if he left the battle-field alive. She complied with his wish, and his presence in the field turned the tide of victory. When the general, Saad, returned, he told his wife how the battle would have been lost but for an intrepid stranger—whether a

F

In the invaders of Syria we behold an army, as already remarked, such as the world had never seen before and seldom since. The command which they received from Abu Bake was at once stringent and enlightened. They were not to mutilate the dead, not to slay old men, women, and children. Not to cut down fruit trees, not to kill cattle unless they were needed for food; and these humane precepts served as a code of laws of war during the Mohammedan career of the conquest. And this, be it remembered, among Orientals who had always been remarkable for their disregard of human life. A Christian may almost blush to contrast it with some

---

man or angel, he knew not. He suspected, however, that he was either the immortal Enoch or St. John the Baptist. His wife then told him the truth. He immediately released the old toper from his fetters, and promised he should never be punished again for drinking wine. He would leave his punishment to Allah who, doubtless, would be merciful to so brave a soldier. "Nay," said Abu Midjan. "I drank as long as I knew that the scourge of an earthly magistrate could cleanse me of my sin, but now I will cease to drink, because I fear the chastisement of God." Dr. Weil, in his "Lives of the Caliphs," has preserved a fragment of one of the songs of this old wine-bibber—that, indeed, which got him this punishment:—

> "When the angel of death shall close my eye,
> Let my grave be 'mid the vines on the hill,
> For, though deep in the earth my bones may lie,
> The juice of the grape shall nourish them still.

> "Oh, bury me not in unfruitful land,
> Or death to me will be terror and gloom,
> While fearless and bold I shall wait his hand,
> If cheered by the hope of the vine's perfume."

Christian conquests. With the massacre of four thousand five hundred Pagan Saxons by Charles the Great; with the order of the Papal Legate to the too conscientious scruples of the general who was sent against the Albigensians, "Kill all. God will know His own;" or the conquest of Mexico and Peru by the Spaniards; and the sack of Magdeburg by Tilly.

But to select an example. Jerusalem has been taken twice by the Mussulmans and once by Christian conquerors. The first event happened in the year A.D. 637, when it surrendered to Omar, the third Caliph, after a long siege. On this occasion no property was destroyed except in the inevitable operations of the siege, and not a drop of blood was shed except on the field of battle. Omar entered the city with the Patriarch, conversing amicably about its history. At the hour of prayer, and being invited to worship in the Church of the Holy Sepulchre, he refused, for fear his descendants might claim a similar right, and so the freedom of religious worship which he wished to secure to the inhabitants by the articles of capitulation might be endangered.

Again, the city fell into Christian hands. In the year 1099 the Crusaders took it by storm, after a much shorter siege, It was then delivered up for three days to indiscriminate slaughter and pillage. Men, women, and children there was no mercy for, and every crime that brutalised humanity can perpetrate was committed without restraint. Foulcher, of Chartres, a monk, who was present and witnessed the abominations, and whose history may still be read, records the events with satisfaction, and has not uttered one word in condemnation of what he saw. It was a great matter of rejoicing that on this occasion 70,000 people professing the faith of Islam were put to the sword. And we commend this fact to the Christian sympathy and admiration of Mr. Gladstone and those who believe with him that the Turk is " the one great anti-human specimen of humanity," that after they had sought mercy at the hands of the Christians ten thousand of them were put to death in the Mosque of Omar itself.

About a century passed away and the city was again pillaged. In the year 1187 the Moslems returned again, stormed the place and took it. They came then with the burning memory of the atrocities the Crusaders had perpetrated. Godefrey de Bouillon was as hateful to them as Nana Sahib and his companions are to us, and Saladin had made a vow that he would be avenged for the innocent blood that had been shed by the Christians. When the city fell into his hands, however, he remembered the mission of the armies of Islam, and disdained to take vengeance upon the helpless. No blood was shed; the Eastern Christians were allowed to remain in the city unmolested;

the Franks to ransom themselves and leave the place.

We are diverging, however, from the point which we started with, namely, the rise of Islam and the principles by which it was guided in its attack upon the world. For it must be remembered that not the Christians only, but the Sabians, idolators, Jews, and, indeed, all who were not "true believers," were dared to try their faith and sword with Islam. Our interest, however, rests mainly with the Christian nations, whose condition is universally admitted to have been deplorable.

It does not lie within the scope of this work to say anything of the faith as held by the most orthodox Christians of that time, or of the corruptions that had crept into the most celebrated ecclesiastical institutions. Society, as a whole, was eaten out with the leprosy of sin; as Isaiah once said, "the whole head was sick, the whole heart faint; from the sole of the foot even unto the crown of the head there was no soundness in it." From the palace to the hovel the consciousness of moral responsibility seemed to have departed.

Lord Beaconsfield has sketched this life-death with his usual felicity. He says:—

"Creeds, customs, statutes, changing like a dream,
The dying dream of dim decrepitude,
Feeble and nerveless, wild at once and weak,
A change that had no order and no aim,
The shifting of a sufferer in his cell,

> Who varies torture with his restlessness.
> And all was pitiless, silent, vague, and dull,
> And Nature and Society both seemed
> Alike exhausted ; like an ancient pair
> Upon the winter of whose latter days
> Pour thick the shrivelled leaves, that gusty Sorrow
> Drives from Misfortune's tree. A piteous scene ;
> War brought no glory, Peace bore no delight ;
> The hand forgot its craft, the eye its skill ;
> All sense of beauty, and all sights of love
> Dropped off and died ; the temple of high thought
> Raised by the lofty souls that conquer Time,
> Each hour some falling column told its fate ;
> The very soul of man seemed changed and struck,
> For even his crimes lacked vigour, though most vile ;
> The craft of woman and the eunuch's spite ;
> All honour, justice, love of fatherland ;
> And holy faith, and household chastity ;
> And the high soul that will not breathe a slave,
> And all for which men strive, or live or die,
> All withered from the face of the wan earth ;
> While mid the ruins of her palaces,
> Discrowned Empire, with her toothless threats,
> Sat like a beldame on a churchyard tomb,
> At whom the urchins scoff."*

It was over the polluted inheritance of those people that the Moslem armies made their way. Not to take vengeance, nor to take for themselves the luxuries of other nations, for this they were sternly forbidden to do. It was a strange and savage boast of Attila, "the scourge of God," that the grass never grew where his horse had once trodden. But of the Mohammedan conquests it would rather be true to

---

* See "The Revolutionary Epic," Book I., p. 9.

say that, after the first wave of invasion had swept by, two blades of grass were found growing where one had grown before. Like the thunderstorm, they fertilised while they destroyed, and from one end of the then known world to the other, with their religion they sowed the seeds of literature, of commerce, and of civilisation.*

ISLAM, then, meant not only a faith—it was an inspiration. The word signifies the delivering up of *self*; and with the article Al, it is restricted to the meaning of delivering the whole being up to God. The man who joined "the faithful" believed he entered a brotherhood of immortal life. The present became a speck, a mere sun-beam in the eternal day that was before him. He had entered the dwelling-place of the Most High, where Allah is all in all, and had left behind him, beyond the threshold, the cast-off garments of the Evil One. Selfishness, cowardice, which is one of its worst forms; the love of the world, the love of luxury,† and the fear of death—

* See J. Bosworth Smith's "Mohammed and Mohammedanism," p. 155, a book that should be read by all who desire to understand the religion of the Moslems.

† The self-denial of some of the companions of the Prophet was rather amusing.

The inhabitants of Hems once appealed to the Caliph Omar, and brought the following accusations against their Governor:—1st. That he never granted an audience before sunrise; 2nd. That he never attended to anyone during the night; and 3rd. That he was altogether invisible for one whole day in every month. When Omar desired him to explain his conduct he replied, "In the first place, all those belonged to the devil, and were therefore condemned, abjured, and despised. The Moslems fought then, as they still do to this day, and as they will do to-morrow, with Allah and Paradise before and Satan and Perdition behind them. It was this electric faith, which Mr. Gladstone calls a blind fatalism, that made the Mohammedans conquerors. It was opposed by the relics of saints, and such other holy gear and tackle, just as the right honourable gentleman's friends, the Serbs, have been fighting of late under the protection of the Holy Virgin, the Panslavonic Council having sent a wooden image of her from Moscow, which the Serb kissed, and then cut off his fingers rather than fight, evidently thinking the demon before him in the form of a Turk a much more trying customer to deal with than Satan in the rear.

---

as I have no servant, I am obliged early in the morning to knead and bake my bread; secondly, during the night I pray to God and read the Koran until sleep overtakes me; and thirdly, as I have only one upper shirt, I cannot show myself on the day I wash and dry it." Omar made him a present of 1,000 dinars, the greater part of which he gave to the poor.—WEIL.—(*Foot-note to " Ockley's " History of the Saracens," p. 266.*)

BOOK II.

BULGARIAN AND OTHER ATROCITIES.

BOOK II.

CHAPTER I.

RAISING OF THE CURTAIN.

We are about to describe the first few scenes in what bids fair to be the greatest tragedy the world has ever witnessed. There have been great slaughters before our time—the invasions of Europe from the time of Xerxes downward have been sanguinary enough, but this great struggle is entered upon with weapons of destruction that were never dreamt of in those days—cannon, throwing their shells for miles and miles away, until one may say, this is the patent age of new inventions for killing bodies, and the mind is appalled at the multitude seemingly ordained to destruction. "All is prepared—the fire, the sword, the men, to wield them in their terrible array. A human hydra, issuing from its fen, goes forth with nerves and sinews bent to slay;" and here, before the actors begin their several parts upon the stage, we may take a brief glance at the *dramatis personæ*.

The Turk is the victim to be sacrificed. They put no garlands upon his brow, as those did who offered the blood sacrificed upon the altars in ancient times; he is not even the scapegoat bearing away the sins of the people—it is a case of brutal murder and plunder, without the shadow of an excuse for "the deep damnation of his taking off."

Behind the victim stands the principal executioner, "the best of cut-throats," Russia; next to her stands Austria, willing to dabble her hands in Turkey's gore, provided she can profit by it. Russia has pride, ambition, and the consciousness of a great mission in the world, and even her brutality is redeemed, in part at least, by this ennobling idea. Austria, except her noble Magyars, is a "mudlark," and will dip her sleek, fair hands, in mud or blood, provided she gain something by the operation. Side by side with Turkey, and opposed to those, is Great Britain, who wants nothing, and who fears nothing. She will not allow a friend to be put to death. She has also vasts interests—some purely humane, others commercial, and, above all, those that are imperial. The freedom of mankind, the freedom of commerce, the protection of her Indian Empire, cause her to adopt a resolute policy upon the subject.

Behind these, pale, cadaverous, hungry, and blood-stained, are the Secret Societies; not the Garibaldini—they are neither assassins, nor robbers, nor yet cut-throats, but purely and simply enthusiastic Republicans, ready to labour, to fight, and if need be, die for their cause.

We have now to call the reader's attention to a series of events, which, although seemingly having no connection with one another, yet all converge together in bringing about the insurrections, massacres, and wars which have for some time been desolating some of the fairest provinces of Eastern Europe.

Early in the year 1875, the Emperor of Austria visited the southern provinces of his empire. He met the Prince of Montenegro, and received him, not as a vassal prince, as he really was and is, but as an independent sovereign. Among other honours he conferred upon him a colonelcy in an Austrian regiment—a polite way, let us suppose, of getting him into Austrian as well as Russian pay. The Russian reply to this move of Austria has lately been given by the proclamation of Prince Milan King of Servia.

Taken by itself, this act of Austria's would not perhaps go for much; but looked at in conjunction with other circumstances, it becomes a matter far beyond court etiquette; it is, indeed, an invitation for a vassal prince to rebel against his lawful sovereign.

On the 2nd of July in the same year Consul Holmes, writing from Bosnia-Seraï, supplies Earl Derby with the following information:—

"I have the honour to report to your lordship that there is disturbance in the Herzegovina. Early last winter, some 164 of the inhabitants of the district of Nevessin left their homes and went into Montenegro. After remaining there some months, however, they petitioned the Porte to be allowed to return to Nevessin. The Governor-General advised the Porte to reply, that as they had chosen to leave their country for Montenegro, they might remain there. The Government, however, decided to accept their request, and allowed them to return. Shortly afterwards they appeared in revolt, declared that they were oppressed, refusing to pay their taxes or to admit the police among them, and they have been endeavouring by intimidation to cause their neighbours in the surrounding districts to join them. The Mutesarif of Mostar invited them to come to that place to state their grievances, which he assured them would be redressed, but they refused, and the Governor-General tells me that they cut to pieces a man quite unconnected with them, who had gone to Mostar to seek redress for some grievance, and threatened with the same fate any within their reach who should do so in future."[*]

---

[*] "Turkish Affairs," No. III., p. 1.

The actors in the tragedy now come upon the stage.

Acting-Consul Freeman, in a despatch to Sir Henry Elliot, gives the following sketch of the leader of the movement:—

"This movement originally began at Kozaratz, in the district of Griedor, and is said to have been at the instigation of a certain Pezzia, a renowned brigand in Bosnia some eighteen years ago. He was in prison at Constantinople for many years, and was then sent to Bosnia to complete his term of imprisonment. On the way, however, he managed to escape from the police who had charge of him, and has since then lived in Servia. The insurgents at first intercepted the road from Banialuka to Gradiska and cut the telegraph wire, but they appear soon to have retired from that vicinity, and telegraphic communication has been re-established. They have burnt several of the guard-houses placed along the frontier, and put to death a non-commissioned officer and two privates of a frontier regiment whom they found in one of them; also one or two other acts of violence and murder are said to have been committed by them. Their number, which is variously stated at figures varying between 300 and 600, is slightly on the increase."*

Another incident, and by no means an unim-

---

* "Affairs in Turkey," No. II., pp. 3 and 4.

portant one, had occurred a little earlier. General Tchernaieff, who had been something of a hero in Central Asia, left the Russian army and became editor of the *Russki Mir* at Moscow, putting his sword and pen at the service of the Pan-Slavonic Secret Societies.

It will, perhaps, surprise the reader to know that there never was any insurrection in Herzegovina at all, in the proper sense of the term. There had been no agitation and no complaints. It came like thunder from a clear sky. The Turkish officials, the Austrian, and indeed all the Foreign Consuls treated it as a trifling matter that might be put down by the police. It was, however, soon discovered that it was almost a case of dementia or hallucination. The Christian people were persuaded to pull down their houses, murder their Turkish neighbours, the young men to join the army of rebels, the women, children, and feeble folk to take refuge in Montenegrian or Austrian territory, and all this was done under the full persuasion that a Russian army was advancing toward them and would build a marble palace for every hut that was destroyed.

Writing to Earl Derby, March the 9th, Consul Holmes describes how the brigands proceeded on their way. He says:—

"Before they reached these villages, however, the disaffected peasants, who had forced and persuaded many others to join them, had attacked and captured a caravan of twenty-five horses on the road from Mostar to Nevissin, belonging to some merchants of Serajevo, laden with rice, sugar, and coffee, which they carried off to the village of Odrichnia. At the same time they murdered and decapitated five Turkish travellers, named Salih Kassumovich, Marich, Samich, Ali of Nevissin, and another whose name is not yet known, a native of Hrasné. One of the insurgents, named Tchoubaté, at the head of about 300 followers, drove away forty Zaptichs placed in the defile of Stolatz, and separating into small bands have for the moment intercepted the various roads in the neighbourhood." *

We have thus seen the opening of the tragedy. A fortnight later a telegram from the Austrian correspondent of the *Standard* at Vienna gives the following information from the same source :—

"The English Consul, Mr. Holmes, has arrived in Mostar, and has himself witnessed the horrible cruelties committed by the insurgents. One band set fire to a Turkish house, and before the eyes of the parents they stuck the children on spits and and roasted them alive. Then the parents were massacred."

The reader will be pleased to know that not one drop of *Christian blood* was shed in the whole of those transactions.

It may not be quite so pleasant to be informed

---

* "Turkish Affairs," No. II., p. 10.

that Earl Russell ex-Prime Minister of England and one of the authors of the Crimean War, the man who threw down the gauntlet to Russia in the House of Commons, declared war against her and prayed that God would defend the RIGHT, sent £50 and his best wishes to the *insurgents* (?).

CHAPTER II.

THE PLOT THICKENS.

Lying between Montenegro and Servia, and bordered also on other sides by Bosnia and the Austrian province of Dalmatia, is the poor and stony province of Herzegovina, and it was here, as we have seen, that the great tragedy was opened.

The first actors who came upon the stage were quite worthy of the cause in which they were engaged. We have Imperial, Christian, and polite Austria, with her high pretensions to science, art, and civilisation; with her grand Exhibition of the industrial products of Europe then in full blast, the first to move. And there was Holy Russia, as they call her at home. And with higher pretensions than either of these—there were the Secret Societies, who, in their bad way, have gone in for a "NEW MORAL WORLD." And these sublime stage managers contrived to put their piece upon the boards with the lowest villains and cut-throats in Europe for the actors.

"I don't mean to reflect," for imperial personages are far above reflection; and the directors of Secret Societies, who whisper their guilty secrets in the dark, have little communion with those who dwell in the light. Still, a quiet, modest man, who would rather go to perdition with a few noble, honest, truthful souls than take the highest seat in the Valhalla of Liars, may ask those august and imponderable beings, why it is that *they never by any possibility tell the truth?* I have, I believe, read every telegram, report, and despatch that has been issued from the first commencement of this dreadful business, and I defy anyone to bring me two telegrams, or one despatch, or State paper that has been issued, either by the Montenegrins, Servians, or the so-called "Herzegovinian insurgents," that is not a piece of mendacious lying. To use Byron's simile, they lie like epitaphs, and seem utterly incapable of telling the truth, even when it would be their interest to do so.

Again we ask, why is this? and hope some philosopher, German, or of any other nationality, will answer us. We warn him that he must be of the transcendental order of thinkers, for, to ordinary mortals, the thing "passeth all understanding." Swedenborg tells us that, in one of his interviews with certain spirits in Hades, he saw some who could not bear the idea of there being anything good or true. The sight of Innocence and the realisation of the idea of Truth in the mind threw them into spasmodic convulsions and gave them the most fearful pains and torture. Hence they never mentioned it, nor even thought about it. The great Seer does not, in this instance, do what he frequently does, tell us what country those spirits came from; but it is plain enough now—they were Serbs, with a sprinkling of diplomats and emissaries of Secret Societies among them. Well, I suppose they have enlisted under the banner of the Father of Lies, and are all " chips of the old block."

In contrast with this, the Turk has been truthfulness itself. Only one of his despatches or reports has, that I know of, ever been questioned. The report of Edib Effendi has been impeached by Mr. Baring. We shall discuss that matter in its proper place. In the meantime one is glad to know that those with whom our interests are so inseparably connected are above the lying, slandering, and truce-breaking which characterise their enemies.

There was, then, no insurrection, in the ordinary sense of the term. They had nothing to complain of, nor, indeed, did they complain; and no people could be more surprised than the peasants and villagers of Herzegovina were when strangers came and told them they must rise in revolt against their lawful sovereign. When the affair got into the diplomatic correspondence and newspaper reports there was an outcry raised about the taxes; but this was soon settled. It was shown that some districts never had paid any taxes to the Turkish Government at all, and that all the others were two years in arrear. When the matter was submitted to the Sultan he at once forgave all the arrears and reduced the future imposts by two-and-a-half per cent.

An attempt was also made to get up a sensation about the persecution of the Christians respecting their faith. But the "religious grievance" was a greater failure than the taxes. The Turk gives full religious liberty to every form of faith, and it is amusing, in looking over the despatches of our Consuls, to see how hard some of those Christians were working to get up a cause for offence. There is no complaint of any interruption of their worship, or of annoyance of any kind. Nay, more; their faith exempted them from service in the army unless they chose to enlist, but still they, or at least their pretended friends, were not satisfied.

One of those serious causes of dissatisfaction is given in a despatch from Acting-Consul Freeman to Earl Derby, dated Bosnia-Seraï, 2nd March, 1876. Our Consul is, as the Puritans used to say, "greatly exercised," and evidently writes with a face straightened to the gravity of a gravestone over the astounding intelligence which he is about to convey. It is "that a new minaret is ordered to be added to the chief mosque of this town. It is to be built higher than the existing one, that it may command the orthodox church and steeple." Mr. Freeman has evidently lost his way in going abroad. Why does he not come home and advocate the levelling of all our steeples, for they certainly overlook the Dissenting chapels? But we suppose lofty architecture is not an offence anywhere but in Turkey.

"But to proceed, for there is more behind." The Turks, like the English, have a law which prohibits peals of bells from being placed and rung in steeples of Dissenting churches. "Many people are inclined to think the matter of church bells is of very little consequence," says Mr. Freeman; not so our diplomatic body; so from Lord Derby the affair is relegated to Sir H. Elliot at Constantinople, and by him brought before the Grand Vizier, who does not care a rap about the matter, but would like to know what Mr. Consul Holmes thought about it, and in reply that gentleman writes:—

"As a matter of fact, the Christians have long enjoyed religious liberty, except in the matter of using bells; but whatever has been conceded to them seems of little account if this privilege is denied, which they appear to consider as the symbol of their religious liberty and the proof of its recognition. Were the use of bells allowed they would have nothing more to complain of in the matter of religious freedom, and would then begin to feel confidence in the good intentions of the Government. The more intelligent Mussulmans here seem to be quite disposed to concede the point, and Haidar Effendi himself promises to carry it out."

One is pleased to know that those tremendous efforts were not made in vain. Three weeks later Mr. Freeman was able to report:—

"I am glad to be able to report that since Sunday last a bell has been rung at the orthodox church in this town, and the Mussulmans seem to have treated the matter with the utmost indifference. It is true it is a very small one, and the sound produced resembles rather the striking of a clock than the ringing of a bell, but now that a beginning has been made the Turks will get accustomed to the sound, and probably make no opposition to eventually a larger and more sonorous bell being used."*

So much for the persecution which the Christians were receiving at the hands of the Turks: let us now see what their brothers in faith were doing almost close at hand.

The reader must fully realise this fact, that foul and detestable as the plot was and is, the insurrection in Herzegovina and the subsequent massacres were all got up by Austria, Russia, and the Secret Societies with one simple object, THAT THEY MIGHT HAVE AN EXCUSE FOR INVADING TURKEY! and we have now to show how the infamous design was worked out.

---

* See "Affairs of Turkey," No. III., p. 18, 59, 68, &c., &c.

For this purpose a swarm, which called itself an army, was, as we have seen, got together in the spring of 1875, and placed under the command of a notorious brigand who had escaped from his jailors. He seems to have received his commission in Servia, and in a short time was in command of a force, variously estimated from three to six hundred followers. They are described by one of our Consuls as "brigands, jail-birds, and gipsies." A pitiless lot of wretches who ought to have been hung to a man. That was the army of patriots, and this is how they went to work to accomplish their nefarious purpose.

Herzegovina was nothing to them; for the purpose, however, for which they were sent it was geographically the best position in the whole Turkish Empire, and had evidently been selected by more clever brains than theirs. They could always get out of the way of the Turkish force which was sure to be sent against them, since they could retreat into the Servian, Montenegrian, or Austrian territory, and there laugh at their pursuers. When the Mussulmans came they found a village sacked and burned, with every evidence of brutal outrage, and started in pursuit. They had no difficulty in following the trail, but it was to find that the enemy had retreated into some neighbouring territory.

The first thing the rebels did was to recruit their army, and they did this in a way at once ruthless and brutal. They surrounded a village, killed all the

Turks, removed the women, children, and infirm and aged into some neighbouring territory, and forced the young and able men who were capable of bearing arms, on pain of instant death, to join their band. In this way, and by drawing to it the dregs of the earth from other quarters, a force was raised, which in no long time was estimated at nearly nine thousand men.

This legion of cut-throats WAS PAID BY RUSSIA, DREW ITS SUPPLIES, GUNS, AND AMMUNITION FROM AUSTRIA, AND HAD ITS HEAD-QUARTERS IN MONTENEGRO!

This, however, was only until Servia should be ready to take the field.

The scene of their operations was visited by Consul Holmes in August, 1875. The whole thing had been a puzzle to everybody except the chief actors who had got up the tragedy, and who, in theatrical language, had resolved to "pile up the agony." So Mr. Holmes, in company with some other Consuls, went to see the leaders of the insurgents, and, if possible, ascertain what they wanted?

He did not see them. Some subordinates put in an appearance, but the only certain thing he could get from them was, that they would not lay down their arms. Those innocent Consuls seem to have been quite unconscious that the people they were talking to were mere puppets, and that the wire-pullers were away in Moscow, Bucharest, St. Petersburg, and Vienna.

Lay down their arms! I have no doubt the rascals snickered over the notion. This horrible work was the realisation of their dream of happiness. They had wandered on the hills out of the way of the Zaptiehs, cold, and hungry, had pined in the fever dens of large cities, and done "their time" in dull drudgery and starvation in jails and prisons. And in those times they had vowed to commit crimes more horrible than any they had yet perpetrated, and here was the opportunity to gratify every lust of their life. There were Turkish women to be ravished, men to be tortured and killed, and babies to be roasted in the flames of their father's homesteads all around them. Why should they lay down their arms when Servia and Montenegro would offer them shelter, one great power supply them with money, and another supply them with the tools necessary for the carrying on of their infernal calling?

Here is a peep at a little of their handiwork. Consul Holmes writes:—

"On the 12th instant (September, 1875) I arrived at Nevessine, with my French and Russian colleagues. We found all the eastern part of the town towards the plain, and all the bazaar burnt and in ruins. Dead bodies were lying in various corners unburied; and we noticed the head of a boy in one of the streets blackening in the sun. A little Turkish girl was brought to us, wounded in the throat, and we were told that an insurgent was on the point of cutting off her head when she was snatched from him by another less bloodthirsty, and allowed to escape. We were told that, as far as could be ascertained, some fifty or sixty persons perished on both sides during the attack."

After stating very fully the particulars of his journey, and giving it as his opinion that the insurgent had no substantial grievances to complain of, and that the whole plot had been arranged by Servian agitators and accomplished by force, he says:—

"The mass of the inhabitants, unarmed, had no choice. Their homes were devastated and their lives threatened, and they were ordered to follow their leaders. And now the ruin is such that those who wish to submit cannot. They have no homes to go to, and the armed bands threaten all who breathe a whisper of submission. These bands are all formed of a mixture of people from different parts of the country, and all mutually watch each other to prevent any combination to submit.

"The ruin and devastation in the plain of Nevessine and along all the Dalmatian frontier, and wherever the insurgents have passed, is piteous to behold, and renders any satisfactory arrangement more hopeless than it would otherwise have been."[*]

---

[*] "Turkish Affairs," No. II., p. 27, 29.

CHAPTER III.

THE CHIEF ACTORS ON THE STAGE.

We may drop the Panslavonic army of "brigands, jail-birds, and gipsies" for a short time, and welcome some august personages upon the stage. One cannot sup perpetually on horrors, and it is a relief, if only for a time, to escape from the company of those pioneers of a "new moral world," and breathe the serene and sweet atmosphere of diplomacy. Besides, as Byron represents their parent on a certain occasion, so they are a little tired of their work,* and for several reasons want rest.

---

* " Even the very devil,
On this occasion his own work abhor'd,
So surfeited with the infernal revel.
Though he himself had sharpen'd every sword,
It almost quenched his innate thirst of evil.
(Here, Satan's sole good work deserves insertion;
'Tis that he has both generals in reversion.")—
Vision of Judgment.

They want fresh supplies of arms and ammunition from Austria, cash from Russia, a few recruits in the shape of trained military officers, and, above all, they want time, to use their own phrase, "FOR TURKEY TO BLEED TO DEATH."

Under date of May 28th, our Consul at Ragusa, Mr. Monson, writes to Lord Derby to inform him that he has had a long interview with some of the insurgent chiefs, of which the following is the result:—

"On my putting the direct question as to what were the present intentions of the insurgents, they replied that nothing was positively known. It was clear, however, that their best policy would be to arrange with Russia and Montenegro that the armistice, if agreed to, should not begin till July, and should then last for two months, by which time the return of the inclement season would forcibly suspend military operations, and give more time for Turkey to "bleed to death."*

The insurgents wanted time, if for nothing else for feasting, and dissipation, and intrigue. They had stolen most of the sheep, cattle, pigs, and poultry in a large district, and removed it into Montenegro, where they were going to roast, eat it, and wash it down with stolen wine. How they must have laughed over their cups when

---

* See "Affairs of Turkey," No. III., p. 224.

they saw how the great ones of the earth were about to take up their cause!

As hinted before, the Turks could make nothing of the affair, and for a time treated it with contempt. They were, however, soon awakened to a sense of the perils of their position, and realised, perhaps, for the first time for centuries, that there really was a vast conspiracy, aided by two great military powers, to crush them as a nation!

To a brave man, or a brave nation, such an idea has but one result: the nervous hand grasps the sword. As the prophet said, when he saw the Assyrian coming, "as the wolf on the fold," furbish the spear, make ready for the battle, and, spite of all the difficulties which surrounded him, the Turk drew his sabre, and cast away the scabbard, not for conquest, but for a life or death grapple with his foes, and appeared in the field in such force that his enemies paused, and thought slow depletion the surest method of dealing with him, believing, with Falstaff, that "discretion is the better part of valour." Hence, the wily and cowardly suggestion to "bleed him to death."

There is a characteristic, one might say almost racial phrase in this suggestion. An enraged and noble foe would have flown at the neck, bent on cutting the carotids and jugulars at once. The sneak and brigand love to torture their enemies; to open a vein where they can without hazarding their own vile lives, and gloat over the agony of their victim.

And it needed the native courage and sublime trust in God which characterises the Moslem to look the difficulties which surrounded him in the face without terror. His credit had been destroyed by Russian agency, so that he could not borrow another shilling on the Exchanges of Western Europe. Abroad he was discredited; at home things were worse.

There was something nearly approaching anarchy in the capital. The Sultan, poor Abdul Aziz, was ill, almost insane. Excitement, and, it is said, dissipation, had exhausted the nervous energies, and left an intellect, never very strong or brilliant, a wreck. He lived in perpetual dread of being burnt. The sight or name of fire alarmed him almost to frenzy; he was, indeed, a monomaniac.

To appreciate the misfortune which it is to a nation like Turkey to have a Sultan in this condition, we must understand what his position is in the State which he governs. The Sword of Islam is in his charge. As commander of the Faithful he is the leader of two hundred millions of Mussulmans, a great brotherhood, whose fortunes and lives are one.

The keystone of this arch then was utterly rotten when the destruction of the empire was resolved upon in the cabinets of Emperors and the secret council chambers of Panslavonic and Omladina committees; and Count Andrassy comes upon the stage to gain time for the cut-throats of Herzegovina, Bosnia, Servia, and Montenegro to carry out their infamous designs.

The telegraphic wires flashed all over Europe the welcome intelligence that Count Andrassy was preparing a programme for the settlement of the Eastern Question. The news was received with gladness in Western Europe, and day after day, and week after week, politicians, journalists, and capitalists watched with eager expectation to see what the mountain would bring forth. The feeling was very different among the so-called insurgents, who were feasting and carousing on their spoils in Montenegro and Dalmatia, and raising shouts of ribald laughter over the whole performance.

It is impossible to suppose that Lord Derby was ever for a moment deceived in this matter. A careful study of his despatches convinces me that he looked upon it from first to last as an infamous, if not an infernal farce. This feeling breaks out again and again in his despatches, and it is due to him to say, that from first to last he never took any part in those machinations, but maintained the character of a prudent, truthful, and brave Englishman.

It will be seen from what was just now said that the insurgents, as they are called, wanted a two months' armistice; their friend Andrassy obtained six weeks for them, and in the meantime produced his famous Note.

Amidst the throes of Europe the mountain was delivered—not even of a mouse, for that animal can be seen and described; it was not a chameleon, for that assumes various colours, and this could not be said to have any—it was an insignificant cuttle-fish that had discharged its ink bag in such a way as to defy any one to determine what its shape and proportions were.

Earl Derby sums up the Count's Note in the following form, which we give in our own and not in his lordship's words:—

Full and entire religious liberty: which already existed in the Turkish Empire, and did not happen to prevail to the same extent in either Austria or Russia.

The abolition of the system of farming the taxes —a thing which, so far as the insurgent provinces were concerned, as we have seen, had no meaning.

The third proposition was, that the produce of the direct taxes in Bosnia and Herzegovina shall be employed in the interests of those provinces. The Count must have written that sentence with a sardonic grin upon his face, since the government of those districts is an absolute annual loss to the Porte of *a hundred and nineteen thousand piastres.**

---

* See Mr. Holmes' despatch of Sept. 28th, 1875, " Turkish Affairs," p. 29.

Well may our Consul add :—" In Bosnia, almost to a man, the population would refuse to be annexed to Servia or Austria, and they have never dreamt of independence, which, from the nature of circumstances and the state of education, is impracticable. They also only wish to be Turkish subjects." The next point which Count Andrassy suggests is a specia commission composed of an equal number of Mussulmans and Christians to execute those *reforms*. (?)

And, lastly, the amelioration of the condition of the rural populations, a matter in which his Excellency might safely count upon the sympathy of every man and woman in Western Europe.

As Rabellais said on his death-bed, " Drop the curtain—the farce is over;" and the assassins for whom a six weeks' armistice has been gained are ready to start again upon their evil work.

Consul Holmes, writing from Mostar to Sir Henry Elliot, raises the curtain again upon the cut-throats of the piece. The block-houses in Piva were in want of provisions, and as baggage animals could not be obtained, two thousand Turkish soldiers started to re-victual the places, each man carrying from eight to ten okes of grain. The ground was covered deep with snow, and thus rendered impassable for any but hardy and daring men. Mr. Holmes then proceeds :—

" The insurgents had assembled in the Douga Pass, expecting that the object of the expedition was to re-victual Nicksich, and so missed the convoy, which arrived safely in Piva. The officers, having met no rebels, took no precautions on their return march, and the soldiers straggled through the passes without any order, when they found they were surrounded by insurgents, who occupied, as usual, the rocks on each side of the road. Scarcely any resistance was made, except by one Bosniac battalion, which fought heroically, and brought off the General, Selim Pasha. The mass of the troops, throwing away their arms, fled towards a small stream, usually fordable, but they found it impassable from the melting of the snow. There they were huddled together, and were absolutely butchered by the insurgents. It *is said* THAT 800 NOSES WERE CUT OFF, AND MANY SOLDIERS WERE CARRIED AWAY AND DROWNED." *

Another object was gained by the Andrassy move, and in the same despatch we have the following choice piece of information :—

" The Slav press is more active than ever in endeavouring to prevent pacification or submission, and I was told by my Italian colleague at Ragusa that a certain Wessilitzki Bozidorovich, a Russian agent, told Baron Gondolo, one of the heads of the committee at Ragusa for succouring the destitute, THAT HE WAS CHARGED WITH INSTRUCTIONS FROM ST.

---

* See "Affairs of Turkey," No. III., p. 54.

END OF THE ANDRASSY FARCE. 117

Petersburg, and furnished with any amount of money to push on the revolution."

So passeth away the Andrassy farce, "full of sound and fury, meaning nothing" but a breathing time, during which the assassins have sharpened their thirsty swords, and can now enlarge the circle of their abominations.

CHAPTER IV.

KISSING AND SMITING.

THE negotiations then having failed, as it was always intended they should do, we must look again at the stage, where the curtain is about to rise upon another scene. The insurgents had been supplied with all they required, and except bringing about the Bulgarian atrocities, may be said to have done their bad work. The next phase is WAR—not with the Great Powers. The quarry is not yet ready for the eagles to swoop down upon it; the kites, ravens, and vampires are, however, preparing to sally forth, and we must first take a look at them.

It is a singular thing, and one which will doubtless interest the psychologist, although it fills the lovers of truth with loathing and disgust, that during the whole time those preparations for war were being carried on, every party opposed to Turkey professed the greatest friendship or loyalty towards her. Russia declared herself friendly, and paid the insurgents to desolate her territory. Austria was "most friendly," but provided arms for the insurgents, and has now equipped Montenegro for war.

Our Consul at Ragusa has for some time been informing Lord Derby and Sir Henry Elliot of the form in which Austrian friendship is exhibiting itself there. In one despatch we are told that the insurgent chiefs have been supplied with all the munitions of war that they require, and that those have been passed on to them by the Austrian authorities of the port. In another despatch we are informed that 14,000 rifles, with a large quantity of ammunition, had been sent into Montenegro "as provisions." Then we are further told that batteries of artillery had been sent by the Austrian Consul in the same direction.

This was how the Great Powers showed their friendship.

The Prince of Montenegro, who has always been with the insurgents, who has participated in the plunder, even to the hundreds of Turkish heads, and noses without heads that have been brought into his dominions, is quite horrified at the suggestion that he harbours any treacherous designs against his suzerain. The Prince of Servia also is almost devoutly loyal; even when he went to war with his troops he professed the greatest regard for the Sultan; and to crown all, the brigands whom Consul Holmes met on the Dalmatian frontier desired to be considered perfectly loyal subjects. He says:—

"They repeatedly declared that they were, and wished to remain, faithful subjects of the Sultan, taking off their caps at the mention of his name."*

It would weary the reader, even if we had the time or inclination, to wade through the long series of official despatches, in which the conduct of Montenegro is displayed. It seems as though almost in despair an agent had been sent, Major Gonne, to visit Montenegro, and, if possible, gain some positive information for Her Majesty's Government as to what was really going on there. And Sir A. Buchanan, writing from Vienna, April 24th, 1876, in a despatch to Lord Derby, says:—"Your lordship will doubtless regret to learn that he (Major Gonne) is already under the impression, from what he has seen and heard, that the war is virtually carried on by Montenegro." †

A despatch from Consul Holmes, dated Mostar, two days earlier than the preceding, is worthy of careful attention, since it gives us an insight into the *modus operandi* of this loyal Prince and his people.

In a despatch to Sir Henry Elliot he says:—

"I have the honour to inform your Excellency that Moukhtar Pasha has returned to Gatzko without having been able to succour Nichsich. He reported having had six encounters with the insurgents whom he reckons to have amounted to 7,000, aided by as

---

* See "Turkish Affairs," No. II., p. 28.
† See "Affairs of Turkey," No. III., p. 102.

many more regular Montenegrin troops. Ali Pasha has received telegrams also from Trebigné and Ragusa informing them that bodies of Montenegrins had marched to assist the insurgents, so that it would appear to be certain that some thousands of Montenegrins really did take part in the opposition offered to Moukhtar Pasha, though I imagine the number of 7,000 to be exaggerated. Ali Pasha thinks that Montenegro desires to acquire Nichsich and its rich plain; but he says that, if she gains her object, Turkey would not be able to retain or occupy the Duga Pass, and that the Herzegovina would, in future, be at the mercy of the Principality. He seems to think the pacification of the Herzegovina will not take place without war with Montenegro as in 1861.

"Ali Pasha declares, with truth, that the chiefs of the insurgents are nearly all inhabitants of the quasi-independent districts of Piva, Baniani, Zapzi, and Montenegrins, who do not represent the sentiments of the real inhabitants of the Herzegovina, and of whose interest and desires they are entirely careless. These individuals who have nothing, and who side entirely with Montenegro are those to whom Baron Rodich vainly counsels submission, but the masses of the poor, destitute, refugee inhabitants of Nevessine, Trebigné, Stolatz, Bilekia, Liubinic, and other places, have no voice and no opportunity to declare their wish to return to their homes.

"Why, is it asked, did the practically independent people along the Montenegrin frontier join the rebellion? Why have they, in conjunction with Montenegro, done all the fighting? Why will they not lay down their arms? The universal reply is, because they obey Montenegro. In fact, all seems to depend on Montenegro, and it becomes more and more evident, in spite of all declarations to the contrary, that the Prince, sheltering himself behind protestations of neutrality, is, in reality, playing a most treacherous part, and rendering pacification hopeless." *

The Turks were naturally angry at this state of affairs, Earl Derby and Sir Henry Elliot sick of the lying by which they were attempted to be imposed upon, were ready to support the Turks in bringing Montenegro to her senses. Russia, however, here comes to the rescue of her pet principality, the scene of many of her machinations against Turkey, and plainly lets it be known that any attempt to check those Montenegrian ravages would be treated as a *casus belli* by her.

In a despatch from Lord A. Loftus to Earl Derby, dated St. Petersburg, April 30th, 1876, he says:—

"Prince Gortchakow then informed me, in reference to the communication I had made, that, under the circumstances he had related to me, and

---

* "Affairs of Turkey," No. III., p. 114.

in view of the menacing attitude which the Porte still continued to observe towards Montenegro, he could take no further steps in regard to inducing the Prince of Montenegro to maintain his neutrality, nor indeed could he answer that the Prince of Montenegro may not be forced by circumstances into action."

Here it will be seen that the Prince adroitly changes the relative positions of the parties; the murderer is transformed into the victim. It is Montenegro, not Turkey, that, according to him, is entitled to sympathy.

In another despatch, dated the same day, Lord Loftus gives us a piece of information which shows that all the massacres, conflagrations, and wars, that have hitherto taken place, had been foreseen and, as financiers say, discounted by the St. Petersburg Cabinet.

He is speaking of the Montenegrian and Servian preparations for war; the work of Prince Gortchakow and Count Andrassy, aided by their subordinates, and refers especially to the outrages already perpetrated:—

" There can be no doubt, said his Highness, that in such an event THE INSURRECTION WOULD ASSUME MUCH LARGER PROPORTIONS, AND A FLAME WOULD BE KINDLED IN BULGARIA, EPIRUS, THESSALY, AND ALBANIA, which the Porte, with its weakened resources, would be unable to extinguish; and the Christian Powers of Europe, awakened by public opinion to the call of humanity, will have to interpose to arrest the effusion of blood."*

It will thus be seen that the Bulgarian outrages, as well as the declaration of war, by Servia and Montenegro, had all been contemplated, and their probable effect discussed by the Cabinet of St. Petersburg, some time before any of them took place.

The Prince of Montenegro, then, is at open war with Turkey. He sends his troops, so Sir Henry Elliot tells Lord Derby, in battalions of six hundred men. The commanders and majors of those battalions are called commanders and pod-commanders; they receive pay. The remaining officers, non-commissioned officers, and men, live as the Scotchman did, upon what they can pick up.

When they start on an expedition, each man takes with him potatoes and bread, if he has any, and a reserve of provisions is carried by women, if they have no baggage-horses. It is a good thing to have friends in such needy circumstances, and we are told that the Austrian committees have provided surgeons, ambulances, beds, and medicines, in the villages all along the frontier. And not to be behind his ally in beneficence, we are told, "not to overtire those poor people, his Highness takes care to change

---

* "Affairs of Turkey," No. III., p. 143.

them at the end of each expedition, or when their provisions are exhausted." *

Neutrality, as interpreted by Russia and Austria, simply means that Turkey shall meet her enemies with her hands tied.

We must now take a brief glance at what was going on in Servia at the same time; for Prince Milan and his cabinet have become greatly alarmed and excited. It is true that they had no grievance whatever against Turkey. They were left alone to govern their petty state as they pleased, and were only asked for a trifling tribute, which they did not pay. Nevertheless, they are greatly excited. In meeting the Assembly in 1875, the Prince opens his address to the Skupstchina by telling the gentlemen assembled that "our frontier populations have lately been disturbed in their domestic calm. Some, indeed, have been forced to leave their fields, and take up arms to guard the security of the country on our southern and eastern frontiers."

His Highness in this instance makes use of a happy and felicitous expression: those people had "been forced to leave their fields and take up arms;" yes, by brigands, jail-birds, and gipsies, many of whom had come from his own territory.

The Prince makes another point in his address; in saying "This state of things, if prolonged, would

---

* See despatch Sir Henry Elliot to Earl Derby, "Affairs of Turkey," No. III., p. 1.

end by becoming intolerable." Quite so, your royal Highness; just as you and your kingdom are becoming intolerable on the face of this earth.

A reply, worthy of the occasion, equal alike in its boasting, hypocrisy, and mendacious falsehoods, was returned to the Prince by a deputation from the Skupstchina, in which, among other things, they say:—

"The Servian nation, which has redeemed this dear country with its swords and blood, is mindful of the words spoken by your Highness in a Proclamation in 1872, 'that it would be a sin to lose the smallest portion of this heritage of our fathers, and it is little enough to our credit that we add nothing to it.'

"These words are engraved on our hearts. The times are serious no doubt, but no less serious, Sire, is the will of the Servian people to rise to the height of the occasion.

"Wherefore, the Skupstchina declares hereby solemnly, on behalf of the Servian people, their readiness as a nation to defend their fatherland and its liberties, and to preserve inviolate the inheritance of the great Milosch and of our fathers; there is no sacrifice which Servia is not ready to make on the altar of the country. At the voice of your Highness the entire nation is ready, as one man, to present itself to defend our native soil." *

* "Affairs of Turkey," No. II., p. 20.

It is hardly necessary to remind the reader that no one (except Russia and Austria) desired to take the smallest portion of Servian territory, and that the Turk, at all events, never intended to attack either their lives, liberty, or inheritance.

They were, indeed, the puppets, screaming on their own small stage. The wire-pullers were in the cabinets of St. Petersburg and Vienna, and the secret committees of Moscow and Bucharest. They are dolls—most of them wooden-headed—who will, when the prompter has done with them, be cast into the fire.

CHAPTER V.

PREPARATIONS FOR MAY DAY, 1876.

EVERY nation has its special day when some event was either accomplished or intended to be perpetrated. We keep our 5th of November in memory of an event that never happened, for although Guy Faux has been tolerably well blown up, he did not succeed in performing a similar feat for the English Parliament. "Black Friday" is well remembered in Lombard Street, and, indeed, we have many black days in the English as well as in the European calendar, but of all those none is so dark, or likely to be followed by more tragical consequences, than the first day of May in this present year. The new era of crime, it is true, did not commence on that day, but it was fixed by the Panslavists as the hour for commencing one of the most fearful butcheries the world has ever seen—the expulsion of the Turks from Europe, the slaughter of four million and a-half of human beings.

It has been the fashion for some time past to talk much of the progress of civilisation and of the influence of Christianity in ameliorating the condition of mankind. Nay, more than this, we have among us an influential body of men, principally clergymen of the Church of England, who are justly esteemed for their piety, learning, and social position, who are anxious to bring about a union between our own and the Eastern Church, which, whatever name it may have merited in other times, is now Russian. We invite those gentlemen to note the matters contained in this and some of the following chapters, and before sending missionaries to the Mahometans and heathens again ask themselves whether it might not be as well to think of converting some churches to Christ rather than of converting people to this Russian form of ecclesiastical worship.

This Russian and Turkish is essentially a Religious War, and it is forced upon the Turk in this form: EVERY PRIEST AND SCHOOLMASTER throughout the Slav portions of the dominions of the Sultan is *ex officio* a member of the Pan-Slavonic Secret Society. The Turk, therefore, whether he would or not, cannot help beholding in every priest who ministers at the Greco-Christian altar a rebel and a conspirator, leagued with assassins; and in every teacher of the children in their schools, and the school itself, a nursery for revolutionists. It is precisely as though every Roman Catholic priest in England, from Cardinal Manning down to the most humble of his flock who wears a cassock, and every schoolmaster or teacher, from the professor in the college to the lowest teacher in their ragged and reformatory schools, was an affiliated member of the Fenian Brotherhood. We all know that the English are the most patient and law-abiding people on the face of the earth, and most of us know also that if such a state of things existed here, and one session of Parliament passed without the whole thing being extinguished, the Gordon riots were child's play in comparison with what would happen during the next month. Every school would be razed to the ground, the chapels burnt, and an end put to a state of things intolerable beyond human endurance. The Turk, then, is the Englishman of the East, and one may say of him what one of another race is by Shakespere said to have uttered: "Hath he not eyes, hands, organs, dimensions, senses, affections, passions? fed with the same food, hurt with the same weapons, subject to the same diseases, healed by the same means as a Christian is?"

The following is the programme of those Turkish Fenians for their performances for the 1st of May, 1876. It is taken from Mr. T. Baring's report:—

"To destroy as much of the railway as possible, including the bridge at Ouzoun Keupni.

"To burn the rolling stock at Sarembey.

"To set fire to Adrianople in a hundred, and to

Philippopolis in sixty places, and also to burn Sofia, Tatar-Bazardjik, Tchtiman, Isladi, and a number of villages.

"To attack the Turkish and mixed villages, and to kill all Mussulmans who resisted and take their property.

"To occupy certain important points, such as Avrat-Alan, Kalofer, Tchoukourlou, &c.

"Bazardjik to be attacked with 3,000 men, and the Government stores seized.

"The rising to be general and simultaneous.

"Such Bulgarians as refused to join in the insurrection to be forced into it, and their villages burnt."

The train had been laid for this infernal consummation with the cunning and malignity of demons. Orators had been sent to the Christian churches to preach vehemently against the Mussulmans, and give warning of a general massacre of all within the pale of Islam; and they had adopted the same tactics in reference to the Moslems. Mr. Baring gives the following example:—

"It is somewhat curious to note that at that time certain mysterious 'hodjas,' who constantly frequented the mosques of Eski-Zaghra and other towns, were loud in their denunciations of the authorities for showing what they declared to be a culpable leniency towards infidels, whose intention it evidently was to destroy the Mussulman faith, and they called upon all good Moslems to rise and massacre the unbelievers. One of these apostles, becoming objectionably demonstrative at Slimnia, was arrested, and, upon being submitted to personal examination, was found to be no Moslem at all. This incident speaks for itself, as it is not difficult to devise from what quarter this pretended 'hodja' had his instructions."

Where were those "hodjas" trained, and who paid for their education and maintenance, and supplied them with funds for the prosecution of their infamous propaganda? The reader is aware that an intellectual man, master of several languages, well read in Mussulman and Christian ethics, and who can only be detected by a *personal* examination, is an expensive article. Such a man is in request in more congenial spheres, where men of learning and culture assemble. What, then, could induce him to make his appearance in the Turkish mosque of an obscure village to incite a multitude of simple people to murder their neighbours? There must be large present pay, and hope of great things for the future, before such men could be induced to engage in such a cause.

For in this case we are not dealing with fanatics, but calculators. They have not entered upon the work as mistaken philanthropists or enthusiasts. Theirs is a question of mechanic and of brute force. Make the Christian and Moslem kill each other, and we will enter into and take possession of their estate. That is the Alpha and Omega of the Panslavist's creed and aims.

Such, then, was the programme for the First of May, in the year of our Lord 1876. That bright day was to be one of arson, robbery, and pillage. Murder most foul and horrible was to follow, and all this at the instigation of a foreign and what pretended to be a friendly power.

We asked just now who paid for all this? and the reply is not far to seek. IT WAS RUSSIA. She paid for every firebrand, provided every sword, and maintained every cut-throat who was to carry out the infernal work. We shall show presently that precisely as the SECRET SOCIETIES spread and acquired power in the same ratio was there a wild cry for money in Russia, and various wild schemes were propounded for getting it. And we commend to the holders of her stocks and other securities this fact, that in no long time the State will be utterly bankrupt; but more of this anon.

Turkey then was in precisely the same position last April as England would be to-day if France were spending millions in aid of the Fenians in Ireland; had supplied the torches which were to burn down Belfast and other fair cities, and paid mercenaries, armed to the teeth, to "wipe out" the English from the Green Isle. What would be likely to happen under such circumstances was forcibly expressed by Mr. Alderman McSweney, late Lord Mayor of Dublin; speaking in the Town Council a short time ago, he said:—

"The Turks had done that which would be done to-morrow were the Fenians to get the ascendancy in this country, and lead the people of this island into revolution; or were the people of this country to be advised and led by the Fenians, the consequences would be atrocities, deeper atrocities, more villainous than ever occurred in Bulgaria."

The sickle of Death was thus made ready. Let us now look at the harvest which was cut down.

CHAPTER VI.

BULGARIAN AND OTHER ATROCITIES.

WE come now to the discussion of a subject, not only tragically painful in itself, but one which in its consequences has nearly upset the policy of Great Britain, shaken our foreign alliances, and compromised the reputation for wisdom and patriotism of some of our greatest statesmen.

In speaking of those Bulgarian atrocities, let it be understood at the very outset that no man in Europe looks upon them with greater horror and detestation than the writer of this book. The heart is sick with agony in reading the accounts that have been written of them, and the whole is not yet told, for the chronicle of the Christian atrocities perpetrated on innocent Turks has yet to be published. We have consequently only half of the ghastly story, nor, perhaps, a thousandth part of the horrors that may yet be perpetrated in Eastern Europe.

But the most terrible portion of the whole affair is, not that in a moment of fanatical frenzy, Christians killed Turks, and Turks took their revenge in the only manner that seemed possible to them; it is, that the whole matter was planned, arranged, and carried out as a portion of a scheme that calculated on a thousand murders for every ten that were committed. The schemers, as remarked in a former chapter, sat in the conclaves of Secret Societies; but they had associated with them generals and soldiers in thousands, princes, statesmen, and diplomatists; patriarchs, archbishops, bishops, and priests, who were ready to bless their banner and sprinkle with "holy" (?) water the assassin's knife and dagger. The whole plot was their handicraft, and if their end had been attained the holocaust would have been so great that the mind is appalled at its contemplation. And yet those sleek, learned, and polished gentlemen have had no anathemas showered upon their heads. Mr. Gladstone, Mr. Lowe, and the Duke of Argyll, as well as the Radicals who have been vituperating the Turk, have not one word to say of those by whom the offence came. Mr. Gladstone is perfectly ready to-morrow to shake hands with General Ignatieff, although it is well known in diplomatic circles that he is one of the principal men of the Moscow Panslavonic Council, and that he and they are covered as with a mantle with the blood that has been shed in Bulgaria, and wrapped in that crimson robe, covering them from head to foot, they meet with no reprobation. The thousands of murdered innocents whose blood crieth from the earth against them, as those that John saw of old, who, with agonised faces raised to Heaven, said, " O Lord, how long?" are unheeded. Yes, how long? how long shall this empire of lies and blood, those schemes from which God and all goodness is banished, be allowed to afflict this earth of ours? I am no prophet, and as Amos says, " neither am I a prophet's son;" but I do know, that the triumph of the wicked is like the burning of thorns under a pot, and that the day is not far distant, when truth, like the stone that was cut out of the mountain without hands, shall smite the gigantic imposture and cause it to fall like the image in Nebuchadnezzar's dream and leave a shattered wreck behind; until Time, like the sea—that great chemical laboratory which always transforms the putrescence of earth into higher forms and more useful substances—shall have transmuted this mass of evil, as the exuviæ of the Reptile Age have left us the coprolites of this.

We concluded a former chapter with a singular statement made by Prince Gortchakoff. It will be remembered that the Prince said that atrocities such as those that had desolated Herzegovina would, in all probability, break out in Bosnia, Bulgaria, Albania, and other places. It will be seen also from that chapter that the Prince was not speaking without authority; for his own emissaries were travelling over every part of those districts, some disguised as Hodjis, exhorting the Mussulmans to kill their Christian neighbours; while others were visiting the Christian churches and preaching a similar crusade, urging the Christians to utterly destroy the Moslems. Besides these, there were diplomatic agents abroad. Here is a glimpse of one of them, given by the special correspondent of the *Standard*:—

"Another illustration of the but half-hidden workings of Russian intrigue in this country is demonstrated by the following facts, which I learned from a most reliable source. A few days after Montenegro had openly joined the cause of the insurgents two Montenegrin emissaries landed on the Albanian coast near Alessio, one of the most important villages of the Miridites, in order to induce this mighty tribe to espouse their cause. A certain amount of money (Russian money, of course, for in Montenegro the article is rather scarce) was offered to the Miridites, and the prospect of plundering Scutari laid before them. Though a few chiefs pronounced themselves favourable to the plan, and promised their support to the Montenegrin envoys, others discountenanced the idea of such an alliance altogether. The Turkish party even succeeded in forcing the emissaries to retire rather hastily, their retreat towards the place where their vessel was awaiting them being cut off by an armed band. Accordingly, they found themselves obliged to retire on Scutari, where they would undoubtedly have fallen into the hands of the Governor had it not been for the interference of the Russian Consul, who sheltered them in his house and facilitated their escape by night across the lake to their native country. These are facts generally known to Mussulmans and Christians alike here."

We have now come to a point in the discussion of this matter when not only facts, but dates become of the highest importance. The great fact to be borne in mind is, that the Panslavists are now prepared for a more extensive sphere of action; that Servia, as well as Montenegro, is to commence warlike operations; and that the scene of insurrectionary murder is to be transferred from Herzegovina to Bulgaria. The reasons for this transfer are obvious: it would, in the first place, enable the Servian and Montenegrian armies to co-operate against the Turk. But there was a deeper reason than this, or at any rate, another reason. It was well known that the Bashi-Bazouks would not quietly endure the treatment which had been inflicted upon the Moslems elsewhere; and the burning of Adrianople and Philippopolis, with other Turkish towns and villages would lead to an outbreak and the perpetration of all the atrocities which Prince Gortchakoff anticipated.

The whole plan, therefore, of a campaign, such as I believe, for its infernal cunning, machinations, and cruelty, stands alone in the history of civilised nations, was ripe for execution, and that the world should be made to take the Russian version of the affair with all its horrible details, three gentlemen were despatched from Constantinople to take notes of all the proceedings and print them. They were—

Prince Tseretcleff, Second Secretary of the Imperial Embassy of Russia at Constantinople.

Mr. Eugene Schuyler, Secretary of Legation, and Consul-General of the United States of America at Constantinople.

Mr. J. A. MacGahan, Special Correspondent of the *New York Herald* and *Daily News*.

The two latter gentlemen had but lately returned from Central Asia, where they had participated largely of Russian hospitality, were, indeed, steeped to the eyes in Russian "proclivities," and their reports must be accepted as the Russian version, *and no other*, of the "Turkish atrocities." They are conveniently silent upon most of the doings of the Christians, and at least Mr. Schuyler goes out of his way at times to utter the most glaring untruths with regard to them and the absence of "foreign agents," in order, if possible, to conceal the fact that the whole affair was due to Russia from beginning to end. Upon the whole, however, it ought to be said that those gentlemen have done their work well, and will doubtless find Russia grateful. They were called upon to give testimony against the Turk, and bettered by their instructions by adding a number of rumours, as we shall presently see, which have marred, if not entirely destroyed, the value of their evidence as historical documents.

We have now to take another peep behind the scenes. Almost immediately after the outbreak in Bulgaria, the Special Correspondent of the *Daily Telegraph* "interviewed" General Ignatieff at Constantinople. His Excellency was exceedingly communicative, and, as the saying is, "made a clean breast of it." He knew, what was doubted by other officials and non-officials, that the outbreak had taken place, and was perfectly cognisant with all its cruelties. He also advanced this singular statement: "That if the Liberals had been in power in England they would have taken no part against Russia." Mr. Gladstone, Mr. Lowe, and the Duke of Argyll, along with Lord Russell and their Radical followers, have, it is true, said and done much to justify this view; still, as this is a matter which involves the honour and wisdom of some of our most eminent statesmen, we shall refer to it again when speaking of the Liberals and their Eastern policy. There is, however, this significant fact at the bottom of it. The Russian Embassy at Constantinople knew before anyone else that the outrages had occurred, and the Secretary to the Embassy started at once for the scene of the calamity, accompanied by his two American friends, for the purpose of misleading the world as to who were the real authors of the mischief.

Although we shall characterise those Russian reports as they deserve, still we cheerfully accord that they have indirectly served the cause of humanity in a very noble sense. They have dragged into daylight the negative side of the Panslavonic butcheries, and the positive will not, let us hope, be long in coming forward. Mr. MacGahan described what he saw and felt, and did not trouble himself about numbers; and although one cannot help feeling that he is only giving one side of the story, and that in his indignation he is consciously, or unconsciously, misrepresenting the other, giving, indeed, a false colouring to the whole picture; still it is well that the thing should be seen in all its revolting horrors, as the enemy sees it. He is quite right in saying—

"It was a fearful sight—a sight to haunt one through life. There were little curly heads there in that festering mass, crushed down by heavy stones; little feet not as long as your finger on which the flesh was dried hard by the ardent heat before it had time to decompose; little baby hands stretched out as if for help; babes that had died wondering at the bright gleam of sabres and the red hands of the fierce-eyed men who wielded them;

children who had died shrinking with fright and terror; young girls who had died weeping and sobbing and begging for mercy; mothers who died trying to shield their little ones with their own weak bodies, all lying there together, festering in one horrid mass. They are silent enough now. There are no tears nor cries, no weeping, no shrieks of terror, nor prayers for mercy. The harvests are rotting in the fields, and the reapers are rotting here in the churchyard."

Such was the scene. Let us now see WHO ARE THE RESPONSIBLE AGENTS THAT PRODUCED IT? The witnesses fortunately are all in court, and their depositions are filed. The Secretary of the Russian Embassy at Constantinople and Mr. Schuyler are on one side, and affirm that the "bands of insurgents had no understanding with each other, and acted without common plan," and "that there was an absence of foreign agents." Mr. MacGahan says the same thing, but he records what he saw and heard, and there leaves the matter. He certainly abuses the Turk soundly, but it does not appear from his narrative that he would not have spoken with equal reprobation of the Slavs if he had seen what they were doing. He is a model newspaper correspondent, who gives the news and impressions of the day with life-like vivacity, and is, we believe, ready to emend, explain, or retract his statements if subsequent discoveries should show that he had erred. We have, therefore, only the two diplomatists to deal with.

Although Mr. Schuyler was accompanied by the Secretary of the Russian Legation, and the last report is signed jointly by them, still the American diplomatist has to bear the responsibility of all that his name is attached to. We may acquit the Russian, therefore, of everything except zeal in a bad cause. It is different with the other. The question has to be put plainly in reference to him, and without diplomatic verbiage. It is, Is his report, what he characterises Edib Effendi's as being, " a tissue of falsehoods"?

It is useless to disguise the fact that Mr. Schuyler's character as a gentleman, as well as one holding a high position as the representative—second only to the ambassador—of a great nation, is involved in that question. It is put with pain, and the reply is given in sorrow; for I have read his books with pleasure, and admire his great ability and learning. Still, he does not scruple to abuse Edib Effendi, and it is only fair to enquire into the truthfulness of his own testimony.

Mr. Schuyler's supreme object is, to show that the troubles in the Turkish provinces of Europe were spontaneous—the result of local oppression and bad government, and that they were not the work of Panslavonic conspirators and foreign emissaries.

We have already said much upon the subject; let us now call a few more witnesses.

The first whose testimony we shall set against him is Lord Derby, who certainly knows as much about the matter as any man living. Writing to Count Schouvaloff, June 29th, 1876, his lordship says that "Her Majesty's Government cannot regard the struggle as being *either exclusively or principally against local oppression, either religious or civil: it was general, political,* EXTERNAL, *and hence the Roman Catholic Christians took no part in it.*"

Another witness, whose testimony is equal to any that can be adduced on the part of Mr. Schuyler, is the special correspondent of the *Levant Herald*, who was one of the first to appear upon the scene, and who, from his position and attainments, is perfectly conversant with the whole Panslavonic agitation. He ridicules the idea of the Bulgarians rising, or intending to rise, from any oppression, real or imaginary.

"They are," he says, "industrious, peaceful, and a little given to drink, and therefore scarcely comprehended what the teachers of sedition meant by their wild ravings. The insurrection was not the work of a day: it had been long and patiently prepared, by diligent efforts and manifold skilful combinations. Some twenty years ago they were thrifty, sober, industrious, and lived peacefully among the Turks. Religion was resorted to in order to instil into their minds the novel idea of nationality, and

K

hence a national AUTONOMOUS church was created, which rendered them independent of their former spiritual head, the Greek Patriarchate of Constantinople. From the church the propaganda was taken to the schools which were taught by young men, who had been trained at the expense of the Russian Government, in the Bulgarian school at Odessa, and returned home to commence the tuition of their pupils, fully initiated into the theories of Panslavism and the designs of the various Russian and Prague committees. At the same time, emissaries under all manner of disguise scoured the country, preaching up the notion of a large Slav empire under the protection of Russia." Thus were the seeds of discontent and revolt gradually sown among the Bulgarians.

The spring of this year, 1876, was deemed an auspicious time. There was an insurrection in Herzegovina; Montenegro and Servia were about to declare war against the Porte. The Vilayet of Adrianople was almost denuded of troops; there was, therefore, every chance of a successful revolt, and hence the burning of the cities, the destruction of the railways and the massacre of the Turks, was decided upon. Special agents had been appointed to set fire to various parts of the towns on the same day, and in order to gain access into Turkish quarters, Bulgarians entered the service of Turkish families in the capacities of servants. The first glimmer of the conflagration was to have been the signal for the Bulgarians to march in troops to the burning towns and slay all the Mussulmans in the affray. The priests and schoolmasters were instructed to tell the people that the hour of deliverance had struck at last, and that Russian troops in large numbers were hiding in the Balkans ready to come to their help at a moment's notice. They were even told that the struggle could not last more than four days, and that those who fell in the fight would be raised from the dead again on the fortieth day.

Although we have not done with our condensation of the report of the correspondent of the *Levant Herald*, we will add here the testimony of Mr. Baring, who is referring to the same time and circumstances. He says:—

"The foreign agitators, and those natives whom they had succeeded in seducing, seized upon this apparently favourable opportunity to strike a blow; the peasants were deluded into leaving their villages by being told that the Turks were going to massacre them, and the population of the small towns was induced to take part in the insurrection by threats and by the most extravagant promises of foreign aid. The revolution was well planned, but miserably executed. The heart of the people was evidently not in it; and many of them apparently thought that all that was necessary for success was a green flag, with a lion rampant, and 'Liberty or Death' embroidered on it. The insurgents put themselves in the wrong by killing defenceless Turks and committing other acts of insurrection, but the resistance they made when actually attacked was hardly worthy of the name."

Yes, it miserably failed! The orders of the insurgent leaders were incomplete and confused. "The able hand," says the correspondent of the *Levant Herald*, "which had so admirably schemed the whole plot, seemed to be missing. There was also a singular lack of discipline. Thus of the sixteen men who had been entrusted with the burning of the town of Philippopolis nine had deserted. The five or six thousand Bulgarians who were raised in échelons at five hours' distance from the town, waiting for the first flare of the flames to rush into the city, grew frightened at not seeing them, and fancying the plot discovered by the authorities, made for the mountains. Some of the inhabitants of the Christian villages, after killing the few Mussulmans who happened to be there, set fire to the empty villages they came by and fled to the Balkans. Banko, and the other under agents who had been lost sight of, had bent their course, the former towards Sofia, where, a few days later, he was cut to pieces by the Bashi-Bazouks, and the other members of the Panslavonic Committee made their way to other localities in the district of Widdin.

The panic had wildly spread, and the disorder in their ranks was unspeakable. . . . . The Bulgarians, having been deluded by false promises, were enraged beyond measure, and killed all the would-be apostles of independence they could lay hands on. Many a schoolmaster and pope fell victims to their blows.

"The Bulgarian revolt is only one link in the chain of a great conspiracy, which had been skilfully preparing for the last twenty years with the view of detaching its Slav provinces from the Ottoman Empire."*

Yet in face of these testimonies, those diplomatists have the audacity to send out a report "printed for private circulation," in which they say "there was an absence of foreign agents" in those outrages.

Consul Blunt, writing from Salonica 13th June, 1876, says: "Some Servian emissaries, with about thirty insurgents, made an irruption into the mountain district of Malish, and burnt some Bulgarian houses, hoping thus to force the Bulgarians to rise, and massacred some Mahometans." †

But it is needless to cite further authorities upon this subject, so conclude with Mr. Baring's account of the origin and outbreak of those atrocities :—

* Abridged from the *Levant Herald* of July 21st, 1876. See also Blue Book, "Affairs of Turkey," No. V., pp. 20, 21, 22, and 23.

† See "Affairs of Turkey," No. III., p. 324.

"About fourteen years ago the Bulgarian Committee was established at Bucharest for the purpose of fomenting insurrection in Bulgaria, and of wresting that rich province from the hands of the Turks, to add it to the great South Slavic Empire, which schemers in Moscow and elsewhere have decided shall be built up on the ruins of the Austrian and Ottoman Empires. Revolutionary ideas were not, however, at first received with enthusiasm by the Bulgarian people, who are a peaceful race, and who were, moreover, comparatively well treated by the Turkish authorities, who purposely fostered dissensions between them and the Greeks, fearing lest a too good understanding between the great sections of rayahs might be fraught with danger for the peace of the Empire. It was not, therefore, till 1867, during the Cretan insurrection, that the Bucharest Committee thought that the time had arrived for action. Emissaries were dispatched to find out the temper of the people, and to excite them, if possible, to rise; but the mission of these agitators failed signally, and they had to return to those that sent them, with the news that the Bulgarians were not yet fit to be admitted into the bosom of the Panslavic family. From this period to the spring of 1875 the Slav propaganda was carried on steadily throughout the province by agitators and emissaries of every sort; and though, I am positively assured, the Turkish Government was perfectly well aware of the presence of these men, with that *insouciance* for passing events which is one of the chief characteristics of the Sublime Porte, they never made the smallest attempt to arrest them or to counteract the effect of the revolutionary ideas they were instilling into the minds of the people. In the spring of 1875 the insurrection broke out in the Herzegovina. This was an opportunity not to be lost, and the emissaries made great efforts to get up a revolt, and actually succeeded in making a slight disturbance at Eski-Zaghra in the month of October. This revolution, or rather riot, ended in a miserable failure; all who had a hand in it vied with each other in betraying their neighbours, and the outbreak was quelled without the smallest difficulty."

We shall have in a future chapter to speak of Mr. Schuyler and his reports again, and hence have confined our remarks here to the simple question of the value of his testimony, and find it worthless. Prince Tsereteleff and Edib Effendi had the belief that they were serving their country; but this gentleman is either paid for his evil work or "pledges his soul gratis." That I am not singular in holding this opinion of him is clear from Lord Derby's despatches, Mr. Baring's reports, and the despatches of our consuls in various portions of European Turkey.

We may, then, sum up Mr. Schuyler's reports by saying that they are an entire misrepresentation of the whole affair, conceived and drawn up at the instigation and under the influence of the Russian Embassy at Constantinople. No such number of people as he states (15,000) ever perished in the outbreak—probably not even a third of that number. The ravishing and other crimes are more than seven-eighths of them imaginary. That innocent blood was shed, and vile crimes perpetrated, is a fact deplored by no one more than the Turk; but it was the Pan-slavists who caused the crimes, and the lying reports of the atrocities were written at Russia's instigation.*

---

* There are two or three circumstances in connection with these reports which one would like to have explained. First of all: Why was the fact that those two American gentlemen were taken to the scene of the outrages by the secretary of the Russian Embassy, so carefully suppressed in the reports of the *Daily News*, and the *public* report of Mr. Schuyler? And Secondly: Why did those gentlemen speak Russian only through Bulgarian interpreters? Were those interpreters some of the "hodjas" who had been preaching this new Panslavonic Crusade? Doubtless "those whom you know,"—the Secret Committee in Bucharest, who are said to have spent 12,000,000 roubles upon their first year's work, could, if they would, enlighten us upon the matter.

CHAPTER VII.

BULGARIAN AND OTHER ATROCITIES (CONTINUED).

It is exceedingly difficult to get at the exact facts in reference to the actual numbers that perished in those outrages, and equally impossible, in the present stage of the enquiry, to determine what other crimes besides murder were perpetrated. The numbers of the slain have been put as high as 200,000, and as low as about 2,000. It is easy to account for those wild surmises; they are like the fable of the three black crows. Some exaggerated the numbers in pure wild affright; others from a desire to damage the Turk; others recorded them from mere hearsay; while Edib Effendi, in his haste, evidently made an estimation that was below the actual number of those who perished: he seems, however, to have been nearer the truth than anyone else. There are, indeed, no absolute statistics that can be relied upon at all. The main fact lies between Mr. Baring's and Edib Effendi's reports. To accept the Turkish version, we must suppose that their guesses at the number of persons inhabiting the different villages was correctly estimated from the taxation of the people, which can hardly be correct, since the method in which the Bulgarian houses are constructed sometimes allows several families to live in the same homestead.

Again, to accept Mr. Baring's number of 12,000, we must assume two things still more incredible, viz., that those were not villages at all, but that some had 8,000 or 10,000 inhabitants in them, which would make them important towns, especially in a country so sparsely populated as Eastern Europe; and further, that all who were absent when he made his report had been killed. Fortunately, we are in a position to show, at all events, that this latter supposition is not correct. The special correspondent of the *Daily Telegraph*, writing from Constantinople, 7th October, 1876, says :—

"Having just passed through Bulgaria, I have visited many of the places reported as destroyed, and everywhere found the regular troops quartered outside the villages, and a very welcome absence of Bashi-Bazouks. Houses were being rebuilt in all directions, the Turkish Government having given money and timber for the purpose, and the Bulgarians were gradually coming back to their old homes. There is, I am informed, a much smaller number killed than was at first supposed, many persons having hidden themselves in the mountains and the neighbouring towns. Since the regular forces have been in the districts these fugitives have returned. For instance, in the Yeni Keni division, Tatar-Bazardjik, wholly destroyed, with supposed great loss of life, is now entirely restored and inhabited—only forty people being at present missing, and some of these are expected to make their appearance in time. At Outloukeui the same state of things prevails, with this difference, that, unhappily, the missing are in a larger proportion. At Waecarel, near Sophia, I was told that matters had been most exaggerated, no one being killed and only a few houses burned. This village is now full of men, women, and children. Peroustitza is nearly rebuilt; at Avrat Alan the people were receiving assistance, and energetic efforts were being made to aid the inhabitants of Batak.

"Mr. Baring's theory that the insurrection had been carefully planned seems to me supported by sufficient evidence, and I heard details of the rebellion at Otloukeui from Bulgarians who were present, to my mind proving a widely-spread insurrectionary organisation. The Christians tell a more coherent story now the panic has ceased, and there is reason to hope that the actual slaughter may be less, perhaps, than even Mr. Baring, who is still in Bulgaria, computed.

"The trial of the murderers is progressing, and

large numbers of convicted Bashi-Bazouks are sent daily to this city, the Porte seeming determined to bring the offenders to justice.

"I find the Bulgarian higher classes very generally opposed to autonomy. They declare the people unfit as yet for self-government. All they want is an improved administration, the right to bear arms, a reformed system of taxation, and equality before the law.

"With regard to the Bulgarian villages reported to be burned by the Turks in the vicinity of Nissa, the assertion is positively untrue, as I was a personal witness to their destruction at the hands of the Servians, and therefore beg to send to England an unqualified contradiction of the whole story."

The number of the slain, then, is not, and from the nature of the case never can be, known. The same correspondent, in a more detailed report which appeared in the same paper, October 18th, supplies an admirable illustration of the manner in which the vague and exaggerated rumours got into circulation respecting the number of the victims who perished in this miserable affair. He is speaking of Yeni Keui in the district of Tatar Bazardjik, and says:—

"This place is situated on the high road between Tatar Bazardjik and Ichtiman, about fifteen miles from the former. It contained about 1,200 houses, and of these, when I passed through hurriedly, on my way to the war three months ago, more than half were in ruins. I think only one family remained in the place, and that was represented by one individual only, a very pretty, well-dressed maiden, who sold coffee to passers-by. She did not at the time, as I well remember, show any great signs of trepidation, although the road was filled by Bashi-Bazouks who were journeying to the front. But I grieve to say that her love of her race overcame her respect for truth, and she deliberately told me that all the people who lived in the place had been murdered. 'Have they not fled to the mountains?' I inquired. 'No.' 'Are none of them alive?' 'None.' She perhaps had repeated the tale so often, in her wish to shield her hidden friends, that she half believed it herself, and no blush of shame mantled her cheek as she told the well-accustomed falsehood. Yet I doubted her, for the reason that the sole survivor of four thousand people would surely have been more grave on the very morrow of their death: besides which, prowl about among the ruins as I would, I could discover no skeletons, no bodies, no fragments of dress. It is true that she pointed out a convent, where she said some nuns had been killed, and events have proved that herein she told the truth; but the light and airy way in which she spoke of the destruction of the township conveyed to my mind a happy misgiving. Last Wednesday it was my fate to pass through Yeni Keui once more. As we approached the village from the Balkan slopes I looked for the ruins in vain. There was the spot, truly; but thereon stood a thriving village—this was Yeni Keui, without doubt. Was I on enchanted ground? No; the mud walls—Yeni Keui was always built of mud—looked a little fresh. There were at the side of the road, a little way down the village, some ruined cottages—a score, perhaps—and there could be no mistake in my recognition of the damsel who had told me the tale of Yeni Keui's woe. But the streets were full of children and women; men were peacefully working in the gardens; girls were at the well; and there were all the evidences of vigorous life. So I set to work to inquire whence all these contented Bulgarians had come. 'From the mountains,'* was the reply; 'they ran away from the village when the Turks came, and waited there till the regular troops arrived to protect them; and now they have received money and wood to build their houses, fresh plots of land, and are fairly comfortable once more.' 'And,' said I to a number of matrons who stood in the street, 'how many of your friends have you missed?' 'About forty,' was the response. 'When the English chelleby'—meaning Mr. Baring—'was here we thought 150 were killed, but many have come home

---

* The reader will see, by referring to General Tchernaieff's report, *Russki Mir*, to the Panslavonic Council of Moscow ("Turkish Affairs," Vol. III., pp. 127, 128) that large stores of provisions had been hidden in the Balkans. Those fugitives were therefore in no danger of starvation.

now, and perhaps there are others yet in the towns or on the hills.' And this was one of the places in which it was stated that at least 1,000 persons had been brutally butchered. I then inquired into the story of the forty girls who were reported to have been burned in a barn, and I found that it was false."

It is a matter of literary rather than of political curiosity to see how those exaggerated reports of the "Turkish Atrocities" ever got into circulation at all. Everyone knows that things as bad, and even worse, have been done in every quarter of the globe. There was, however, in this case a special reason for creating a sensation, and the Russian hands being too deeply dipped in blood, and their tongues so addicted to lies, that the truth from them would have been the most incredible thing in the world, they resorted to the method of working by proxy. Hence the Secretary to the American Legation of Constantinople undertook the dirty work.

Two things were especially intended to be accomplished by this method of proceeding. First of all, the gentleman was to bear false witness—which he does over and over again—that "the whole insurrectionary movement was of local and not foreign origin." Mr. Schuyler repeats this statement, knowing how difficult it is for any sensible man to believe it; and "I vow that he does protest too much." Mr. Baring treats his assertions with the scathing contempt they deserve. Referring to Mr. Schuyler's statement* that " no Turkish women or children were killed in cold blood, no Mussulman women were violated, no Mussulmans were tortured, no purely Turkish village was sacked or burned, no Mussulman house was pillaged, no mosque was desecrated or destroyed,"* he says:—

"The idea that a person totally unacquainted with the facts of the case would gather from their statements would be that the Mussulmans, without the smallest provocation, had simply fallen on the Christians and massacred them; in fact, that what really did take place at Boyadjikeui took place at every village throughout Bulgaria. I do not suppose that anybody will come forward and deny that the Bulgarians committed the first overt acts of rebellion, and that they shed the first blood. What could be more cold-blooded than the murder of the gipsies and other Mussulmans at Avrat-Alan? It is said the gipsies were going to plunder the villages, but there is not a jot of evidence to prove this intention; and, moreover, is it likely that about 100 men could sack a large and populous place like Avrat-Alan? It has been denied that a single Mussulman village was burnt or a single mosque destroyed, when with my own eyes I have seen the ruins of both. The Mussulmans of Streldja are also undergoing considerable misery. The fact is that

---

* See " Turkish Atrocities," p. 94.

when the revolution declared itself the most indescribable panic seized upon the Mussulmans; they expected an invasion of Servians and Russians, they knew themselves to be in an immense minority, they credited the Bulgarians with courage and fighting power which they certainly never possessed, and they thought that immediate massacre would be their fate."*

And yet Mr. Schuyler has not retracted one of his assertions, although he and everyone associated with him must know by this time that they are utterly untrue.

In estimating the value of those Russian reports, we must take one fact into consideration, which is, perhaps, the key to the whole of them. If the reader will refer to "Affairs of Turkey," No. v., p. 21, he will find, what is recorded in a dozen other places, that the communications of the Panslavonic committee of Bucharest were never signed by any single individual. The words "those whom you know," and the seal of the Central Committee being sufficient to establish the authenticity of the document. When, therefore, the Russo-American Commissioners started from Constantinople, they went into Bulgaria to meet those who were crammed with lies, to make up their report.

It is not necessary to dwell long upon this painful subject; the horrors surrounding it are too palpable,

---
* Mr. Baring's Report.

L

and the lying so palpable that every Christian man would fain believe the whole a horrible nightmare. Having exhausted the catalogue of torture and murder, this American gentleman becomes so prurient that one is amazed at his relating such disgusting things on such wretched evidence. Thus we are told that on one occasion a number of ladies waited upon Mr. Schuyler, and told him they had not suffered any outrage from the Turks, " but," it is added, " they left a paper, which said they had been stripped, and subjected to outrages indescribable and inhuman."

That paper has never been published in any of Mr. Schuyler's reports, and never will be, from the simple circumstance that it came from " those who knew " what was required, and supplied the vile ingredient.

Happily, however, we have one case in which we can test the truth of this Russian catalogue of outrages. The "Bulgarian Queen," as she is called, was for some time a prominent figure in those Bulgarian outrages, and to begin with we cannot do better than give Mr. MacGahan's description of her.

He expected to find, he said, a sort of Amazon, but instead of that, discovered a slight, graceful form, with large hazel eyes, an oval face slightly browned by the sun, and a veritable little rose-bud of a mouth. Her name is Raika, and she is a daughter of a priest in the village of Otluk-Rui, or Panagurishti, about twenty miles from Tatar-Bazardjik. At the age of twelve she had been already remarked for her intelligence and beauty, and a kind of literary club raised a fund and sent her to the American Missionary School for girls established at Eski-Zara.

"Raika remained at this school four years, was an expert pupil, and among other attainments acquired great skill in embroidery. At the end of four years, when she returned to her native village, she was regarded as a prodigy of skill and learning. She now became one of the mistresses in a village school, where she seems to have conducted herself to the satisfaction of everyone."* it is impossible not to sympathise with the poor girl; clever, beautiful and good-hearted, she had, without any fault of her own, drifted within the circle of some of the vilest and worst conspirators the earth has ever seen, and who were only too ready to make use of her for the furtherance of their nefarious designs.

The thing above all others the insurgents supposed they needed was a flag, and Raika, by certain threats and persuasions, was induced to make it.

This piece of her handiwork is said not to have been without its merit. On a groundwork of satin was a huge yellow lion, with its paw on a crescent,

---

* "Turkish Atrocities," *Daily News* pamphlet, pp. 34, 35, 36, 37, abridged.

which it was attempting to rend in pieces, and in Bulgarian the bold motto " Liberty or Death ! "

Whatever scruples Raika might have had in making the flag, her father had none whatever in consecrating it for its deadly purpose. It was accordingly taken to the church, blessed, and, as *Macbeth* would say, " the banner was hung on our outward wall," and the inhabitants resolutely set to work to erect fortifications and to conquer or die under their new standard.

Playing at rebellion, however, and actual fighting are essentially different affairs; hence, when the Turkish troops made their appearance, those who had buckled on their armour to conquer or die threw away their muskets and ran to the mountains. The resistance which they offered was contemptible, and the Turks treated the people, in this case at least, with a clemency they scarcely deserved. Among those who fell righteously was Raika's father, and she herself, being regarded as one of the chief conspirators, since she had been paraded through the streets of the town and formally proclaimed " Queen of Bulgaria," was taken a prisoner and sent to Philippopolis. If this had happened in England she would have had ten years' penal servitude; in America she would have fared still worse ; in France she would have been sent to the guillotine ; in Germany, or Austria she would have been hung; in Russia she would have been beaten to death with the knout;

the "barbarous Turk," however, treated her very differently. She was imprisoned for about two months and then dismissed with pity and contempt.

The whole of these facts are taken from the Russian reports, which also relate a series of outrages, violations, insults, and cruelty, which would have disgraced even Russian jailors; of her being ravished in public, and other matters that it is not necessary to transcribe. Raika herself never uttered a word about anything of the kind, but "those who know" could give all the most minute details with the utmost circumstantiality, and yet the girl herself—who certainly ought to know if anyone does how she was treated—stoutly denied to Mr. Baring that anything of the sort had happened to her, and expressed her willingness to submit to a medical examination that the truth of her assertion might be demonstrated.

But oaths of truthful people, corroborated by medical science, are not acceptable in Panslavonic circles when they refute convenient lies, and hence the brazen testimony of false witnesses is still kept before the public.

It is disgustingly ridiculous to relate; but not a few of those stories of outrageous slaughter originated in the idle boasting of sneaks and cowards. A correspondent of one of our daily papers gives a case in point. A certain Bashi-Bazouk was boasting to him of his prowess, in proof of which he exhibited a dagger covered with blood up to the hilt. He had, he said, killed six people with his own hand that morning. On enquiry, however, it was discovered that he had only killed a goose, and that the blood was that of the innocent bird.

In the "Affairs of Turkey," Vol. III., p. 333, there is a perfect gem of the kind. Consul Read at Rustchuk is very anxious to supply Lord Derby with some information respecting the Bulgarian Outrages, and having no direct information had recourse to stratagem. Doubting the Christian testimony he sought information from Moslems, and learning that one of that persuasion had arrived in the town he engaged a trustworthy Mussulman to pump him. Both the Consul and the agent were deeply impressed with the importance of the undertaking, and record what took place almost with bated breath. The spy says:—

"This morning I went to a café, where a Mussulman was sitting, in company with several Mussulmans of Rustchuk.

"When asked whether he could be called a Ghazi (champion of the faith), he answered, 'I will not speak of what I have done; but when I tell you that even our schoolboys killed their five or six Bulgarians, what can you imagine that I did?'

"He praised the Circassians as having done great things, having as their motto, 'Giaur culsun, vurunuz culsun' ('Let the Giaour die—strike him, let him perish').

" A Bimbashy (Major) present asked him if they had taken rifles from those that were killed. He replied, 'That they had not even a hoe with them, much less rifles.'

The Bimbashy then said that they must have killed innocent people. He replied, 'Yes, very few had arms.'

" Another present remarked that 5,000 or 6,000 must have perished innocently. He answered, 'If you had said 25,000 or 26,000 you would have been more correct.' He added, 'It is a great loss to the country, as most of them were tax-paying people.'

" He also said that at Plevna no Christian could go to his field or vineyard for fear of being robbed or maltreated."

The correspondent of the *Levant Herald*, who passed through the district about the same time, found everything peaceful and quiet; the men were attending to their flocks and herds, and the women working in their fields and gardens. It was, to use a Turkish word, " bosh."

Those " Turkish cruelties" have lately had the full benefit of clergy. First of all a story came from Jerusalem giving a minute account of the arrival in that city of a disabled Turkish soldier who had returned from the war with a beautiful Bulgarian girl, who, he said, had been given to him instead of his wages. He refused £80 offered for her redemption by a wealthy Christian. The story was first told, it appears, by the Anglican bishop of Jerusalem, who gives it as "A new form of Turkish infamies." The Rev. Thomas Smith, who communicates this astounding intelligence to the *Times*, asks with becoming horror, "How many Christian girls and women are thus being sold? Surely the civilised Governments of Europe, especially England, ought not to be indifferent to this new form of traffic in flesh and blood, accompanied as it is by brutal abuse and ill-treatment at the hands of their mendacious allies the Turks, who absolutely laugh, because they think that England is sure to protect them against Russia. Hence the contempt to which the English are exposed in this part of the Turkish dominions, not only from the Christians, but also by the Moslems, who fear Russia, but despise England."

A story, told with such seeming truthfulness, and coming from such high ecclesiastical authorities, was supposed to have some foundation in fact, and hence Lord Derby sent immediately to our Ambassador at Constantinople, who telegraphed to Mr. Moore, Her Majesty's Consul at Jerusalem, to enquire into the truth of the affair. The Bishop was seen, and here is what Mr. Moore says of him:—

"The Bishop says that he overheard some people in the street telling the story, and has no further information. I have myself made inquiries, with no result as yet, and will continue them."

One hardly likes to comment upon such things as

those as they deserve. The Bishop does not tell our Consul who it was he overheard in the street, or how he got the story; neither names, dates, or any particulars could be gained from him, and yet, with this *canard*, or it may be a fact in history which possibly occurred two thousand years ago, we have a clerical shriek over Moslem atrocities, and to crown all the Bishop at last, when hard pressed, admitted that " the statement was inaccurate."

Receiving a beautiful girl as his wages was bad enough, both for the soldier and his paymasters; but Canon Liddon and Mr. Malcom MacColl have something still more strange and horrible to relate. In a letter to the *Times* they assert that they had seen an actual case of impalement, and they give horrible particulars respecting this form of punishment, which they obtained from Bishop Strossmayer, who represented that form of torture as common all along the Bosnian frontier. His Excellency, Musurus Pasha, Turkish Ambassador in London, wrote at once to say that the thing was incredible, if not impossible, in any part of the Sultan's dominions, since by the law of the Empire, torture of any kind was punishable with death to the tormentor, and if the people who inflicted that torture, whether civilians or soldiers, could be found, as they doubtless could be if the thing were true, then their punishment by the Turkish authorities was certain. But this challenge to fact was not accepted. In the usual manner of treating Turkish despatches, several correspondents sent their contributions to the newspapers. One, assuming the story to be correct, spite of the Ambassador's denial, quotes Byron's description of the agonies of the impaled victim. A model writer, however, of this kind, in a letter to the *Times*, says :—

"If all that Musurus Pasha can allege in contradiction to the statement of Bishop Strossmayer, of the Archimandrite Doutisch, of Dr. Liddon, and Mr. MacColl is that the Hatt-i-Sheriff of Gulhané in 1839 abolished the practice of torturing persons to death by impalement, then the contradiction is apparent only, not real. It is one of the complaints, one of the causes of the present insurrection in Bosnia and Herzegovina, that this Hatt-i-Sheriff has never been executed. It remains a splendid promise, without the attempt at performance. It was, indeed, because this Hatt was not enforced that the Hatt-i-Humayoun of 1856 was necessary and was extorted by the Great Powers from the Porte; and because this last Hatt was in the same manner never acted upon, that the outbreak of 1875 occurred."

A greater jumble of nonsense and untruths than this could hardly be put into so many lines. The fact is, no impalements, tortures, or anything of the kind, had taken place at all. The English travellers were, as we shall show presently, mistaken in what they saw; and the insurrection, or rather invasion of the Turkish provinces, has from the first been attempted to be justified by such lies as their Panslavonic acquaintances imposed upon them.

Lord Derby, with his usual promptitude, at once sent to Sir A. Buchanan, our Ambassador at Vienna, and also to Sir H. Elliot, requesting they should inquire into the affair at once. Consul Holmes, as well as the Austrian authorities, investigated the matter on the spot. No such thing had been seen or heard of either by friend or foe. The whole affair reminds one of a sensational article which appeared in a Paris newspaper a few years ago. A correspondent, who had been sent to England, gives a graphic account of an inhuman thing which he himself witnessed. Seeing a crowd collected, and a great fire blazing in a large open space, he proceeded to the spot, and to his horror saw a Chinaman dragged toward the flames, his clothes were torn, he was beaten, and thus outraged cast into the fire. The feelings of the sensitive Gaul were so lacerated that he went from the spot immediately, with the shouts of the glad and excited mob ringing in his ears.

Is it necessary to add that we were at war with China? It was the 5th of November, and Guy Faux was thrown into the bonfire.

But in this case it is not certain that the two clergymen saw even a Guy. A correspondent of the *Daily Telegraph*, who knows the country and the habits of the people, suggests that it was hay put

up in a peculiar kind of rack in use in that country.
The real fact, however, lying at the root of the matter
is that those two clergymen were in a steam vessel on
the River Save; that they saw something through
their glasses, at two hundred yards distant, which
they were told was a Turkish outpost, and something
on a pole, which they were also told was an impaled man. Bishop Strossmayer, who was a long
distance away from the spot, corroborated the
story, and added "that the victims were impaled
with their faces towards Austria, and that one of
them was a woman near her confinement." Oh!
Bishop, Bishop! it was bad enough for a couple of
simple-minded English clergymen, who are so accustomed to the truth at home that they expect to find
it abroad, to be imposed upon; but you, living in
the country, having ample opportunities of knowing
the truth, yet propagate such falsehoods, is simply
atrocious. In our countrymen it was a mistake
that they did not examine the matter with their own
eyes, instead of taking the reports of others on
trust; in you such an assertion is a crime parallel
to the broken word of honour of the Emperor of
Russia relative to the annexation of Khiva. Did it
never occur to your reverence that it is not wise to
leave truth-telling entirely to Consuls and others,
whom you designate "men of the world," and also
that there is, at least we are told so, a remarkable hot
territory reserved for everyone who "maketh a lie?"

CHAPTER VIII.

BULGARIAN AND OTHER ATROCITIES (CONTINUED).

As the heading of this chapter indicates, we intend to glance at other, as well as Bulgarian, atrocities; not for the purpose of justifying any of the outrages that were perpetrated in the Turkish provinces, but simply to show that the Turk comes into court with hands as clean, or even cleaner, than either his Russian or American accusers. With one or two exceptions, the outrages in Bulgaria were committed by incensed people, who were enraged by the slaughter of their women, children, and aged people. One of our Consuls reports that, in order to provoke the Circassians, two of their women were taken by their Christian neighbours, who first cut their breasts off and then murdered them. This, of course, led to reprisals, and thus the social slaughter went on until the regular troops interfered and put an end to the fray. This was analogous to what takes place in all countries whenever there is a servile war or outbreak. It is only when it is indorsed or tolerated by the legal authorities that it becomes a matter of national importance.

A great outcry has been made, and properly so I think, against certain Turkish officers who exceeded their duty in putting down the insurrection, and who received promotion or decorations before the nature of their services was fully understood by the Sultan's Government. Whatever judgment may be passed upon those men, we must take into consideration the almost inhuman provocation which they received, and extend to them the same charitable thoughts which we give to our own officers who so ruthlessly put down the Indian Mutiny.

Now, it so happens, that we have two cases before us which are apt illustrations of this view. We are indebted for the first to Mr. Schuyler himself, who was in Central Asia when General Kauffmann took Khiva. On that occasion the General received a deputation from the Turkomans, who came to offer him not only their subjection, but also such gifts and pledges of their obedience as they were able to afford. They had also this further claim upon his consideration, that they had offered a generous hospitality to all the Russian surveying parties, and travellers, and merchants who had visited them. It must, therefore, have been the desire of the beast of prey, that laps the blood when it can no more devour the carcase of the slain, that impelled Kauffmann to act as he did. He invited certain elders to visit him at Khiva, and, to his surprise, they came. He then informed them that they must pay a contribution of 300,000 roubles (£41,000), that one-third of this must be paid within ten days, and the whole within a month. Now, Kauffmann knew as well as anybody else that those people had not got the money. They are a nomad people, rich in flocks and herds, but without cash. It was impossible to raise it even by the sale of their cattle or their corn, or even the jewels and ornaments of their wives and daughters, for there was no one to buy them.

Fifteen days had been now given for the payment of this impossible sum, and five of the elders were sent back to the tribes to announce the General's decision, the other twelve being retained as hostages until the money was paid. On the very day, however, when the elders were sent away, Kauffmann ordered General Golovatcheff to march and attack the Turkomans, without allowing one of the fifteen days to expire. The order is one of those infernal gems of military literature which it is well to preserve, since they will, in all probability, be to some future generation the same objects of wonder that the remains of the monsters of the earth's reptilian age are to us.

This modern Attila says: — "To follow more closely the payment of the contribution by the Yomuds, I ask your Excellency to start with your detachment for Hazavat on July 7 (19), and to encamp in a suitable place. If your Excellency sees that the Yomuds are not occupying themselves with getting the money together, but are assembling for the purpose of opposing our troops, or perhaps even for leaving the country, I order you immediately to move upon the settlements of the Yomuds which are placed along the Hazavat Canal and it branches, and *to give over the settlements of the Yomuds and their families to complete destruction, and their herds and property to confiscation.*"

The troops, therefore, were despatched, and, in order that their work might be complete and expeditious, Kauffmann added another despatch, in which he says:—" If the Yomuds become submissive stop ravaging them; but keep watch of what is being done among them, and, at the least attempt to migrate, carry out my order for the final extermination of the disobedient tribe."

A fight ensued, and a great slaughter took place, when, finding that the Turkomans really had no money to pay his extortionate demand with, he proposed to take one-half of it in camels, and to help in raising the other half, the women had to strip themselves of all their ornaments and bring them in to the Russian camp for sale at whatever prices could be obtained. Those ornaments have not only been exhibited as rare objects by the Russian Geographical Society at home, but have been making the round of

European exhibitions as trophies of the General's prowess.

Let us take another peep at this organised butchery, and then leave the brutal matter with the loathing which it deserves. An eye-witness says:—

"When we had gone about twenty-five miles from Khiva General Golovatcheff said, before a large number of officers in my presence: 'I have received an order from the Commander-in-Chief—I hope you will remember it, and give it to your soldiers. This expedition does not spare either sex or age. Kill all of them.' After this the officers delivered this command to their several detachments. The detachment of the Caucasus army had not then arrived, but came that evening. Golovatcheff called together the officers of the Caucasus and said, 'I hope you will fulfil all these commands strictly, in the Circassian style, without a question. You are not to spare either sex or age. Kill all of them.' The old Colonel of the Caucasus said, 'Certainly, we will do exactly as you say.'"

Captain Burnaby, in his "Ride to Khiva: Travels and Adventures in Central Asia," gives a still more graphic account of Kauffman's proceedings than that afforded by Mr. Schuyler. After stating the facts relating to the indemnity of 2,200,000 roubles, and that a portion of it had been laid on the Turkomans, with a fortnight given for its collection and payment, he says, p. 260:—

"But the Russian Commander-in-Chief was in a hurry. Instead of waiting the appointed time, he sent out a large detachment under General Golovatcheff to ascertain what chance there was of the payment being made. This General, in order to discover the intentions of the Turkomans, gave an order to his soldiery not to spare either sex or age. Men, women, and children at the breast were slain with ruthless barbarity; houses with bedridden inmates were given up to the fiery element; women —ay, and prattling babes—were burned alive amidst the flames; hell was let loose in Turkomania. And this, the Russians would have us believe, was done to further Christianity and civilisation. This is the sort of Christianity which some people wish to see established in Constantinople. Would they like this kind of civilisation next our Indian frontier? If the Turkomans had been treated differently, they would have paid the tribute to the Russian General. But they are barbarous creatures, utterly unacquainted with that European civilisation which characterises Russian troops. They were so foolish as to be exceedingly angry. Indeed, it is said that later on these poor ignorant Turkomans became utterly lost to all feelings of honour. They actually dared to attack General Golovatcheff's camp at Illyali; but they had no chance against the breechloaders of their foes, and were repulsed with great slaughter."

We need not, however, go so far as Central Asia to find Russian atrocities, which put those of Bulgaria entirely into the shade. Kauffmann, the conqueror of Khiva and the butcher of the Yomuds, the special pet, it is said, of the Empress of Russia, and who received high reward and honours for the perpetration of deeds for which Turkish officials are to be hung, has a worthy compeer in General de Bellegarde, who put down the Polish insurrection in 1863. Here he was certainly not encountering Asiatic hordes or people who had put themselves out of the pale of humanity by the committal of such acts as the insurgents did against the Turks throughout the whole of the disturbed districts in her European provinces. More than this, his executions were not only carried out by the regular army, but were approved of at St. Petersburg, and he himself received both rewards and honours.

If the reader does not sicken over the following catalogue of horrors, it may be as well to go through them, that he may be enabled to appreciate fully the depth of Russia's philanthropy, and the love which is now exhibited for their Slav brethren under Turkish dominion. For the Poles, also, are Slavs, and if they did this to their "brothers in blood," what will they not do with the Turks, if they once have the power, who are aliens alike in race and religion?

The following account of the manner in which

the Polish insurrection of 1863 was put down is taken from the *Dziennik Polski*, a Sarmatian paper of the highest respectability. It was translated for the *Daily Telegraph*, and up to this time has never been contradicted, explained, or even repelled :—

"A name is still pronounced with trembling lips in Poland, when the insurrection of 1863 is spoken of; it is that of General de Bellegarde. His headquarters were established in Radom. He was a lean man of lofty stature, with the profile of a bird of prey. Whenever a few fugitive insurgents were brought before him, and their mothers, betrothed, or sisters plead for mercy to them, he used to exclaim, in his loud, harsh voice, 'They shall hang; *basta!*' or 'They shall be slaughtered, and you with them!' Close to Radom, to the left of the high road to Warsaw, there is a little meadow. Upon this spot Bellegarde had a permanent gallows erected, upon which hundreds of insurgent prisoners were strangled in cold blood. Their bodies were thrust into a large trench hard by. Some women of Radom crept out of the town during the night, and strewed flowers upon the corpses lying in the open trench. Bellegarde heard of this, and forthwith had the pit filled up, ordered a number of Cossacks to compel their horses to trample upon it until it was level with the surrounding ground, and then had the whole meadow covered with dung, so that the place of burial might be totally effaced. The murdered insurgents were Christians, nevertheless; but then, so was their murderer!

"General Siemiatycz-Manjukin had his headquarters at Siedlin. He alone caused 700 human beings, some insurgents, others only suspected of having taken part in the revolt, to be hanged opposite his house. Every time an execution came off he stood smiling and watching it at his window, and always appeared highly diverted when the women standing round the foot of the gallows shrieked louder than usual in their agony. When women came to him to implore his mercy he was wont to beat them furiously with his fists, throw them on the ground, and stamp upon them with his spurred heels. The priest Stanislaus Brzozka held out with a few resolute adherents in the neighbourhood of Lublin, when the revolt was already nearly quelled. He was taken at last, and when he was brought before the General, the latter shouted, 'Give me the scoundrel here!' A fearful scene was enacted. Manjukin seized the priest, struck him with clenched fist in the eyes, knocked his teeth out, flung him down on the floor, throttled him, and trampled upon him. When the poor victim was senseless he was carried out to the gallows and hanged.

"Another instructive example of Muscovite philanthropy was afforded by a colonel, who commanded the Russian forces in the engagement at Fajslawice. At the close of the struggle, which ended disastrously for the Poles, there was found amongst the wounded a non-commissioned officer, who had been an orderly of Kruk. The Colonel, when he heard this, had the wounded man brought to him, and said to him, 'Kruk has always let his Russian prisoners go, and even gave them half a rouble apiece to keep them from starving on their road, so I will also let you go free!' But before the man was set at liberty this monster caused him to be mutilated in a manner indescribable, so that the unfortunate wretch died next day. He caused another wounded prisoner belonging to Kruk's detachment to be twisted up in a number of straw ropes, and then burnt alive.

"A long list of names could be made out of such unnatural monsters from amongst the Russian generals who took an active part in putting down the insurrection. Zarkisoff, Assiejeff, Mednikoff, and Wahl, Count Berg's nephew, figure in the foremost rank of these butchers and mutilators of humanity. How many peaceful chateaux of noblemen and peasant colonies were, without the least pretext, pounced upon, pillaged, and burnt to the ground by these Christian officers! The men were held down on the ground and knouted till they lay mangled and lifeless; the women were mercilessly violated by the Cossacks. General Assiejeff, a Circassian by birth, spread terror wherever he went by the following method of proceeding: When he encountered a carriage or cart upon the public roads he made the occupants get out, and had them knouted till their bodies streamed with blood. If they asked why they were treated in so barbarous a manner, he invariably replied, 'It is only the prologue to my question of, " Where are the insurgents?" Now you will be well disposed to give me an answer!'

"At Wilkomiccz, on Nov. 20, 1863, the insurgent, Stanislaus Kossakowski, who had formerly been an artillery officer in the Russian service, was condemned to be shot. The soldiers told off to execute him, however, aimed so badly that after several volleys he was not yet dead, only horribly mangled. They got tired of firing at him, and flung him, still alive, into a deep ditch full of water, where he drowned. A peasant woman who had witnessed the whole proceeding was so appalled and outraged by the cruelty of this final act, that she broke into loud execrations against his perpetrators; whereupon they seized her, flung her into the water, and drowned her by force."

But America comes forward to express her horror through her Secretary of Embassy at Constantinople, Mr. Schuyler, with his two reports on those Bulgarian atrocities.

A learned and witty Englishman once defined the duties of an Embassy "to lie abroad for its country's good." The good that America is to derive from Mr. Schuyler's labours is not quite clear; but this we may assert, that if lying abroad has any merit in it, he is entitled to run for the next Presidential election.

Did it never occur to Mr. Schuyler that atrocities had been committed in America as well as in Eastern Europe, with less provocation and on a much more extensive scale? General Sheridan is to the great Republic what Kauffmann is to the Government of St. Petersburg. Has his march through the Shenandoah Valley been forgotten? where, with the brutishness of Attila, he destroyed everything before him. Cottages, villas, mansions, towns, libraries, schools, colleges, and even the hospitals and almshouses, were sacked, burnt, destroyed, along with everything that could afford subsistence to the inhabitants. The number of peaceful citizens that were slaughtered has not been recorded; for there was no Turkish Commissioner, accompanied by a Secceesh Secretary of Legation, to point out the spot where the slain had fallen, and produce lying witnesses of horrors that had never been perpetrated.

But this was not the only achievement of "Phil Sheridan," the pet name by which he is known in American circles. He was sent against the Cheyenne and other Indians, who numbered about 15,000, and they never troubled the Government again after he had visited them. The brave, in his war paints; the squaw in her wigwam, the papoose at her breast—all met the same fate. To use the expressive phrase of the American journals which recorded the campaign, "they were wiped out"—their villages destroyed, and their country thrown back to its original wilderness, until the land-jobbers, plug-uglies, and other white trash, should come and take possession of it.

Even while Mr. Schuyler was writing his report, the Congress of the United States was engaged in voting to General Sheridan 2,500 cavalry, together with other resources, that he should undertake a campaign against the Sioux Indians. Sitting Bull and his people could no longer endure the rascalities of the Yankee traders. They had put up with being cheated out of their rations; but when the traders, licensed by the American Government, gave them blankets made of shoddy and devil's dust, which fell to pieces as soon as they were used; muskets which burst as soon as they were fired; and whisky which poisoned those who drank it—the simple savage was roused to wrath, and a scrimmage took place at a trading station between the knaves who sold those wares and their victims. The Indians came out triumphant in the scuffle, and hence a force of some hundreds of men from the United States army was sent against them. They also were beaten, and now General Sheridan is about to go with an overwhelming force against the doomed tribe. They are reckoned about 80,000 in number, but they, too, are to be "wiped out" as the other redskins have been.

Be it remembered that the whites in this case were the first offenders. The Indians wished to live as their brethren in Canada do, in peace with their neighbours; but Yankee cupidity would not allow them to do that, and now the greed to annex their hunting grounds has brought the whole tribe to the verge of destruction, and their extermination is decreed.

Will Mr. Schuyler or his Russian friends shed a tear over these atrocities? We would advise Edib Effendi to accompany General Sheridan in his expedition; he will find much greater need of softening his report of the atrocities which will shortly be perpetrated on the banks of the Yellowstone River, than he ever did for those which took place in the vilayet of Adrianople.

In the trial of those who were arrested, as well as in putting down the revolt, the Turkish authorities have shown a clemency and leaning to mercy's side which will contrast favourably with that of any other civilised nation. When Russia puts down a rebellion, she drowns it in blood. Our officers in India had few scruples in meting out punishments to the Sepoys and other rebels; the French in Algiers showed little mercy; and in a still more analogous case, the Communists of Paris have, since the war was over, been tried, executed, or transported, with little regard to anything except what the exigencies of the case seemed to require. The Turk has tempered justice with mercy beyond that of most, if not any, other nation that has been similarly circumstanced.

Mr. Baring gives this account of a visit paid by him to the court, which had been instituted at Adrianople for the trial of the prisoners who had taken part in the revolt. He says:—

"I was present to-day at the first examinations of some of the prisoners, and to all appearances the proceedings were properly conducted, and Salim Effendi, Ali Bey, and the Chief Mollah of Adrianople have the reputation of being just men.

"A priest, a schoolmaster, a 'Tchorbaji,' and another Bulgarian were brought up while I was in court; their declarations were read over to them, and they were asked whether the contents were true; and, though all contained evidence which would send a man to the gallows before any tribunal, they invariably replied that everything was correct. Their defence was generally the same; they had acted as they had done either from coercion, fear, or sheer stupidity, and they ended by begging for mercy with tears and lamentations."

A few of the worst criminals were executed; some others sentenced to minor punishments; the great mass sent to their native places, and helped to re-establish their homes.

We have heard a great deal about Russian interference in favour of the Turkish Christians. The following extracts from Rufin Piotrowski's work on Siberia, published in 1863 by an English firm, will show how Holy Russia treats some of her own "brothers in blood" who rebelled against her:—

"I now approach a dark episode in Polish suffering. The civilised world will doubt its truth and declare it exaggerated, as it once doubted the horrors committed by Krcczetnikof and Leknly in the days of the Bar Confederation, as it doubted the barbarities of Cherchyn, and listened with incredulity when the story was first told how Catherine II. incited the peasants of Podolia and the Ukraine to massacre and despoil their lords; and how Suwarrow, after the storming of Prague, left no living creature man, woman, or child within its walls.

"The world did not, and still does not, believe that this system was then commenced which drives us away in thousands into the heart of Russian Siberia to fill prisons and casemates; that in Warsaw in the days of Constantine, brother of Nicholas, no Polish family could lie down at night without the fear that, perhaps, ere morning, one of its members might be torn away, consigned to a dungeon, scourged, and tortured with hunger and thirst, so that the confession needed might be wrung from his agony. Sierocinski and four others who had been drafted into the ranks of the Siberian army, were condemned each to 7,000 blows with a stick, 'without mercy.' If any one of the number outlived the sentence he was to be sent to the Nerchinsk mines for the rest of his life. The great mass of persons implicated were variously condemned to 2,000, 1,000 or 500 blows with the stick, and those who survived in some cases to hard labour for life, in others for a number of years to penal colonisation, and others again for military service. . . . .

"At daybreak two battalions of 1,000 men marched out of Omsk, one charged with the execution of those condemned to 7,000 blows, the other with the execution of the lesser sentences. The battalion halted, each formed in double line face to face, leaving passage through the long drawn ranks. The executioner, Galafieyef, superintended the arrangements, and remained with the men who had to give the 7,000 strokes. According to general usage the soldiers charged with such duties are placed closely shoulder to shoulder in dealing the blows, but slightly raise the arm from the elbow and keep their feet together as when standing on parade. The sticks should only be so thick that three can be dropped into a carbine barrel. On this occasion all this was reversed. Galafieyef placed the soldiers at arm's length from each other, made them raise their arms high in carrying out the sentence, and the sticks were thrice the usual weight and size.

"The victims were brought from their prisons to the place of execution. The bloody work was begun simultaneously by both the battalions. From both came the same shrieks of agony. Sierocinski was left to the last, and compelled to witness the fate of his friends ere his own turn came, and he had long to wait for that deadly walk. Then his shirt was stripped from his shoulders, and his hands, according to the regulations in such cases, fastened to a carbine, held by two soldiers, who thus compelled him to keep regular step. The order to march was given. . . . . The priest entered the street of death, reciting in a low voice, 'Miserere mei Deus secundum magnam misericordiam tuam.' Galafieyef shouting frantically, 'Harder, harder! strike harder!' and the submissive tools of despotism obeyed so well that Sierocinski, after walking once down the line and receiving 1,000 blows, fell insensible, weltering in his blood. He was lifted to his feet to fall again immediately; and then a hurdle, prepared for this occasion, was brought. He was bound on it kneeling, and so dragged up and down until his sentence was fulfilled. He had given at first a few shrieks of agony, and still was breathing until the four-thousandth blow, the remaining 3,000 were struck on his corpse, or rather his now fleshless bones. Eye-witnesses assure me that the flesh was cut in strips by the rods, the very bones were crushed and splintered, and the entrails exposed." *

---

* My escape from Siberia, pp. 276, 283, abridged.

CHAPTER IX.

SERVIAN WAR.

WHILST speaking of those Bulgarian and other atrocities, in order to dispose of an unpleasant subject at once, we may as well record here the few remarks we have to offer on that supreme atrocity, the Servian war. In the other districts around the Balkan there were many excuses for the horrors which were perpetrated; hatreds and antipathies growing out of racial and religious causes had already prepared a mass of combustibles that only wanted a lucifer match to set on fire the conflagration. But in Servia nothing of this kind existed. The nation was free by right of treaty from any interference with its political or religious administration, and she set itself free by her own shameless dishonesty from paying the Sultan's tribute. What was done in Belgrade, therefore, was done after long deliberation and anxious thought, and with a definite object.

Long before this a scheme had been elaborated by

the Panslavonic Council at Moscow, which had been submitted to the Servian Government, and accepted by it, and the spring of the present year, 1876, determined upon for carrying it out. That scheme was a very simple one, especially as it appeared on paper.

It was to occupy the passes of the Balkans with a Panslavonic army without a declaration of war by Russia. Make a dash on and capture Constantinople, if possible.

All the steps that had been taken for two or three years past had been directed to this one object. The invasion of Herzegovina by cut-throat bands; the attempt to get up an insurrection in Albania, would, it was thought, cripple the Turkish Government, scatter and occupy her troops, and an insurrection in Bulgaria would so far paralyse all efforts of the Ottoman Government that serious opposition to the march of the Servian army, led by Russian officers, was hardly entertained.

The Bulgarian outbreak was, it will be remembered, planned for the first of May, and to be on the spot and ready to take advantage of those disturbances, General Tchernaieff, who had been some time in Servia inspecting her military resources, reported to his own paper, the *Russki Mir*, that the Serbs were sufficiently powerful to be enabled to take the field with every hope of success.

He commences his singular communication by stating that he proceeded to Servia with the object of making himself acquainted with the real state of affairs in Turkish territories. He went, he says, by way of Kishneneff and the Danube, along the whole course of which, commencing from the Russian frontier to the Servian boundary, committees had been formed towards the end of last year for organising the plans of the Bulgarians in their approaching struggle for independence.

Commencing from Bolgrad (a Bulgarian colony which fell away from Russia and became incorporated with Roumania by virtue of the Treaty of Paris) he everywhere heard the same thing; all was ripe for the impending struggle. The arms that could be bought in Roumania had been acquired; many rifles which had been distributed by the Turkish Government among the Mussulman population had been obtained—how, he does not say, whether by purchase or theft, most likely the latter. "*Large stores of provisions and other property had been removed to the Balkans and secreted under ground.*"

General Tchernaieff then gives an account of his visit to Bucharest, and of the state of military preparation in Roumania. He is not sanguine of their present ability to fight, and hence says:— " Until the people are seasoned under fire all the military movements will be confined to partisan attacks on the communications, consisting chiefly in the destruction of railways, telegraphs, interception of couriers, posts, &c. An attack of Turkish detachments will only be allowed under specially favourable circumstances and under a considerable superiority of strength over the enemy. The first acts of the insurgents have been in strict accordance with this resolve."

He continues his account of his tour through the province Servia, which he describes as a species of ovation from one end of the country to another. "Wherever I passed," he says, "the people shouted 'Long life to our Russian brethren, long life to our orthodox Russian Tsar.'" According to his statement he found that Servia could muster 125,000 well armed popular troops, 200 rifled guns, and 24,000 horsemen for scout and outpost duties. In addition to this the country is able to command 100,000 armed men for the protection and defence of their families and dwellings. He thus calculated on being at the head of a host of nearly 250,000 armed men, only wanting officers to lead them, and those he hoped for, and indeed did obtain, from Russia.*

Tchernaieff himself is a good specimen of a Russian officer; brave, even to daring; clever and polished on the surface; the superficial plating of civilisation, however, is very thin, and hides no greatness of mind beneath it; it is, indeed, nothing more than the lacquer that covers the brutal lusts and pitiless heart of the true Russ. When Governor of Vilna

---

* See "Affairs of Turkey," No. III., pp. 327, 328.

his conduct was so cruel that the Emperor himself recalled him. For a man of his small ability he has won more distinction, perhaps, than any of his contemporaries. In 1854 he gained the cross of the order of St. Anne of the third class for his bravery in the operations on the Danube, and in the following year he was given the order of St. Vladimir of the fourth class for his efficiency at Sebastopol, and received a gold-mounted sword with inscription "for bravery" for his stubborn resolution in repelling the famous attack of the Allied Armies on August 5, 1855. For the capture of Khokand and Nijebek, during the expedition to Central Asia, he was rewarded with the order of St. Anne of the first class, and for the conquest of Tashkend, with a gold-mounted sabre set with brilliants. In fact, the breast of the sturdy Panslavist General is as brilliant as a shop-window in the Palais Royal.

Such, then, is the man who undertook to wage war against the Ottoman Empire.

Wicked and wretched as this war has been from the commencement to the close of its tragic incidents, still it has accomplished an immense amount of good, since it has cleared away the dust and smoke which previously enveloped the affairs of Eastern Europe. It has shown that the insurrection and war did not arise from any misdoings on the part of the Porte and its officials. Whatever its faults and deficiencies, and they are doubtless great, the people themselves showed no great signs of discontent. The Turk may be a dull governor, wedded to old forms and obsolete methods of administration, but taken upon the whole those Bulgarian villagers were well fed, well clothed, well housed, and lightly taxed in comparison with their brothers "in blood and religion" across the Pruth. The Turk is a kind and generally a conscientious master, and the extortions connected with the collection of taxes are usually the work of Greeks and Jews, and it falls as heavily upon the Moslems as upon the Christians.

A gentleman who knows Turkey well, Mr. Farley, says:—" I wish some learned theologian would tell me why it is that men are so much better in all the social relations of life under Mohammedan laws than those of Christianity. It is unheard of for a Turk to strike a woman. He is always tender towards women, children, and dumb animals, and if a dog howl with pain in the streets of Péra you may be quite certain it is not a Turk that has struck the blow. A Turk is truthful and scorns a lie; he is sober, temperate, and never a drunkard or a gambler; he is honourable in his dealings, kind to his neighbour, and charitable to the poor. In Turkey no man, woman, or child can really want bread, much less die of starvation. Can as much be said for Christian countries?"*

---

* "Modern Turkey." By J. Lewis Farley, p. 122.

Well then, the agony column being closed, at least until we come to speak of Turkish reforms, we may advert to another delusion which the war has dispelled; the bravery of the Slav peasant and his impatience to get rid of the Ottoman rule. The cowardice and impotence of the Slav is so abject that his Russian helpers have at late treated him with undisguised contempt, and see in him nothing but the caitiff and the sneak, and do not esteem him even good enough to be food for powder, while the peasants, in their turn, at least those of Servia, regard their would-be deliverers as tyrants and vampires, whom they shot down rather than follow them into a battle where they were promised victory. Poor little Raika's boastful flag bore on it all the courage that the Slavs have displayed in this brief struggle. Even the Czar openly expresses his contempt for them.

But beyond this the great fact has been revealed that the Turk has not degenerated, but still possesses all the qualities which, in their totality, constitutes a soldier. The troops of Osman were not more cool, brave, and determined; the companions of the Prophet more resolute and daring. One who has witnessed most of the battles that have been fought during the Servian war gives the following account of what he saw on one occasion. He is speaking of the battle of Gramada, and of the confidence, bordering on contempt, with which the Serbs and Russians regarded their opponents. He says:—

"There was a line of hills on which the Serbs stood, overlooking the vast plain which runs down to the city of Nisch. On the summit of this ridge was the Servian artillery, behind were the white houses of the pretty little village, with its church, school, and *douane*. As the Turks advanced the Serbs, who might easily have remained inside their trenches, and, in fact, have thrown up many more earthworks, actually came down the slope to meet us. There was no necessity at all for their doing so, but they felt that they were quite equal to the hated wearers of the fez, and they wanted to fight them. Then came a sharp rifle fire, and for half an hour a hardly fought battle, while the Turks were gradually pushing up the hill. The Servians began to discover that their foes were, after all, not to be despised, and they presently sought shelter. But, to their amazement, that, too, was of no avail; up came the Turks, leaving many a man on the hard rocky ground, yet still going on, to the dismay of the blue-coated Serbs, who could do nothing to stop them. Volleys even failed to hinder the Moslems for a moment; and, what was of consequence at this time some guns that the Turks had dragged up to the summit of a neighbouring hill began to play upon the trenches with increased effect. The village of Gramada, too, was in flames, the air was alive with shells, that still-advancing line of Turks was sending up such a storm of bullets that the whistle of the missiles was everywhere heard and the Servians could stand it no longer. They had not expected this. Somebody had told them they were invincible —that the Ottomans would flee before the blue banner of liberty with its cross and its crown, that the hill of Gramada was impregnable, and that no troops in the world could ascend the long, weary slope. Yet the Turks were coming, were close to the trenches, were beginning to cheer and take little runs which would presently bring them into the defences themselves. It was too much. The Serbs felt that they must retreat; and, alas! for all their prestige, these bold Highlanders, who had been compared to Camerons and Campbells, who had sworn to die for their country, and had sung ever so many patriotic hymns, got out of the trenches, and, without more ado, threw down their rifles and retreated. But they were not even then allowed to depart in peace. Those fez-topped children of tyranny actually cheered louder than ever, and, rushing past the trenches into the village, shot down the sons of Servia by scores. Nor were they content with this, for they pursued them that night as far as Derbent, giving many a soldier of Tchernaieff to the crows and the dogs, and only resting when night came on with the intention of doing the like next day—a promise which they carried out with terrible effect. The Servians never liked to meet them after that. Glory at the cannon's mouth was all very well as a sentiment, but at the muzzle-end of Turkish rifle it did not suit General Tchernaieff's troops, and they ran away. On the other hand the Turk continued to make war in his own stolid fashion. Had he been well led, he would have gone straight to Belgrade, and the whole business would have been settled forthwith. As it was, nothing but his own dogged courage saved him. It has always been a beautiful sight to see him go into battle. I never saw a man flinch, although sometimes the fire was terribly heavy and the ground was covered with the dead and dying."

Speaking of another trying occasion, the same writer says:—

"Even the Softa battalions, which had been drilled at Beycos, just opposite our Embassy at Therapia, had caught the true spirit of the soldier, and went into action like men. I well remember a very striking instance of this on August 22. It was towards evening time when Tchernaieff's newly-arrived Russians were trying to fight their way up the face of our position at Resavci. It was clear somebody must stop them, and they were sheltered from our guns by the wood below. The Softas were called up, got into line, 'dressed,' and ordered to double down the hill. For a moment there was comparative silence; nothing but the rattle of musketry and artillery was heard. The priests were gathering inspiration—it was their first battle-field.

Then, with one voice, they shouted 'Allah!' and with this religious appeal they dashed into the woods. Ill fared it with Russian and Serb that day; for the Softas went on, passing between the trees, and searching for the foe, whom, when found, they incontinently destroyed. There was no more cheering till we reached the village at the end of the wood, and the last Serb had fled. Then there was another loud shout, which told that the priests had won their maiden fight, and were victorious. It was always the same; the Turk seemed ever anxious for the fray. The difficulty was to make him keep under cover. I do not think the officers on the other side had any such difficulty. No Turk ever shot off his own hand to avoid the bullets of the infidel."

There is another element, also, which will have to be taken into consideration in dealing with the Turks in Eastern Europe. All the Christians are not Panslavists. The best and most intelligent of them know that New Russia would be but Old Turk "writ large;" that if the latter had chastised them with whips, the former would scourge them with serpents. Hence there was a brave Christian band united with the Osmanli. The same author says:—

"Let it not be supposed, however, that in thus speaking of the Moslem I am attributing to him qualities which other men do not possess. The Christians who formed the two battalions which served under Hussein Pasha, and a banner which bore alike the symbols of the Crescent and the Cross, were quite as brave. The courage of the Turk seemed to be theirs too; they plunged into the fight with all the pluck of their Osmanli brethren, and many a Russ and Serb have been unwilling witnesses to their work. Was it a bad cause which made the Servians fly? or are they a cowardly race, fit only for raising pigs and cultivating tobacco and maize?"

The preceding statements present a condensed report furnished by the special correspondent of the *Daily Telegraph,* published in that journal of the 29th October. The *Standard* of 10th November contains a still more elaborate account of the bravery and endurance of the Turks, of which the following is a brief summary:—

"On the 19th of October, on the attack of the Servian positions near Djunis, the weather was icy cold, the rain poured down in torrents, the ground was covered by slippery yet sticky mud, yet the most perfect order prevailed in the attacking columns, and they climbed the steep hills which they were ordered to carry with the utmost resolution, notwithstanding the shower of shot and shell with which they were saluted. When they reached the summit the Turks, uttering their war cries, dashed fiercely with the bayonet at the foe, who, whether because they were Russians or because, though Servians, they were stimulated by the devotion of their Russian leaders with an unusual access of valour, for the first time stood firm. A desperate hand-to-hand fight took place under the eyes of the correspondent, who seems to have been in the thick of the *melée*. At length the Turks prevailed, the hill was carried; but there was a strongly-occupied village in front to be taken. A Turkish regiment 'rushed onwards without firing a shot, though the soldiers fell in rows,' and the village was soon captured, the Servian artillery having shamefully abandoned their infantry, and the battle soon ceased for the day. The following night was passed by the victors without shelter in the midst of a tropical rain and mud, their sufferings being increased by the piercing wind. Still, they did not murmur, though many of them passed the whole night standing, and it was not even possible to keep watch fires burning, The next day, exhausted as they were with their previous fatigues, and scarcely able to move through the thick mud, the Turks displayed as much gallantry as on the previous day. One part of the enemy's position was carried, but at another point the assailants were brought to a standstill. Though, however, they could not advance, they refused to retreat, and remained stationary under a heavy fire, grumbling loudly, when, towards nightfall, they were ordered to abandon the enterprise, and fall back out of range. The rain had ceased about midday, but the tired soldiers had to pass another night without shelter and lying down in the deep mud. The next day the battle recommenced and, after six hours' obstinate fighting, the Turks, notwithstanding they were thoroughly worn out and the ground horrible, made a decided advance. Theirs was at Djunis 'no sudden outburst of undisciplined valour,' to quote from the eloquent historian of the Peninsular war, but a stern determination to do their duty in the way pointed out to them by their officers. Cold, wet, and want of sleep, and fatigue, which are powerful agents in sapping mere animal courage, all combined to discourage the Turkish soldiers. Yet never in the days of its highest reputation was the Turkish army more formidable. Alike in patience under suffering, in steady resistance and dashing attack, the soldiers of the Sultan were admirable. How, we ask, can the stigma of "deterioration," either moral or physical, be applicable to such men? Neither were the officers less gallant than their men, but led bravely their troops into the thickest of the combat."

The causes already enumerated, and especially the latter, were fatal to the campaign. Instead of taking possession of the Balkan passes, Tchernaieff was driven back into Servia, and pursued from one stronghold to another till nothing remained but an armistice to save Belgrade from falling into the hands of the victorious Turks. The collapse was fearful. The Serb, never gifted with any fine feeling, appears to have been stunned and transformed into a brute. Thousands of the finest men in the country had been killed in battles, or wounded and left to die in ditches. Hundreds, if not thousands of others, had mutilated themselves, rather than risk the chance of death from a Turkish sabre. Towns and villages throughout large districts have been destroyed, the cattle and crops eaten up or wasted, and the bitter winter which has come down upon them with its cruel rains and pitiless frost and snow, will complete the work of destruction, in the death of tens of thousands of people, old men, women, and children, whose eyes will never see the light, or feel the heat of another spring.

One glance more at the principal actors and we may close this painful chapter. And first of all: of the vain, conceited, heartless, shallow-pated little Prince of Servia. When his army was broken, and Tchernaieff bewildered, he went for the first time to visit his troops. He returned to Belgrade on the evening of Nov. 3rd. An eye-witness thus describes his appearance:—

"Prince Milan arrived here at 5.30 yesterday afternoon, travel-stained, haggard, and looking ten years older than when he left. He drove up to his palace door in an ordinary posting carriage, the state of which, as well as that of the team of three half-dead horses, must have been seen to be believed. As he alighted he cast a hurried glance round him, but not one of his Ministers was there to greet him. A few stragglers had been picked up in the streets adjoining the palace, and turned into the enclosure before the entrance portals, but they uttered no sound as their Prince, returning from his army to his capital, stood for a moment, as it were, hesitating upon his own threshold. The captain of his body-guard received his Highness, who, however, neither spoke to nor shook hands with him, but hastened up the steps and into the palace, where the Princess stood awaiting him. In the hall one would have thought that the Russian agent who has urged the unfortunate Prince into this disastrous war, and has moulded his policy in its each successive stage, would have once more crossed the Terassia, as he has done thousands of times for his Government ends, from his consular residence, which faces the palace, to pronounce some well-chosen words of consolation and sympathy to the broken-spirited victim of Russian intrigue —a mere youth, whose amiable qualities, had he been wisely counselled, might have made him a blessing to his people; but M. de Kartzoff had probably received instructions to assume an attitude of reserve. Rats, they say, leave a sinking ship, and doubtless the Prince's evil counsellors have come to the conclusion that the Servian state vessel is in a desperate condition."

At the date of writing this, November 15th, 1876, an armistice has been concluded, and Tchernaieff who, it was fondly hoped would be a second Garibaldi, is being stripped of all his plumes and claims, and his former friends are now holding him up as a monster in human form; a pest to all that is good and free; an incarnation of all that is bad and brutal.

A Russian Radical paper, *Nabat*—the alarm bell, or tocsin—published at Geneva, remarks upon the hero of the Servian campaign:—

"General Tchernaieff, who marked his Central Asiatic Expedition by achievements in comparison with which the worst Bulgarian atrocities of the Bashi-Bazouks are insignificant—General Tchernaieff, lately a Russian journalist, and as such a pillar of the servile press of St. Petersburg, the champion of reaction, despotism, and aristocratic arbitrariness—he and others who have spent their lives in plundering the Poles and depriving them of their nationalty—these are they who have gone out to fight in Servia for liberty and the rights of men. And a nice sort of liberty it will be which these ardent champions of Czarish despotism, these inveterate enemies of the people, are likely to confer upon their clients. However great the heroism of the Servian and Bulgarian nations, however sacred the cause for which the unfortunate Herzegovinese have taken up arms, when it fell into the soiled hands of their present leaders it forfeited its pure and noble character. It simply became a war between Christian

Bashi-Bazouks and Mohammedan Bashi-Bazouks—a war not for the triumph of lofty ideas and popular interests, but for the predominance of cognate systems of oppression."

What might have been sanctified by success was execrated by failure. The *Russian Review* says:—

"Nothwithstanding the sacrifices made by Russia, people at Belgrade are indignant at her behaviour. Our repeated warnings have availed nothing. M. Tchernaieff has insisted upon playing the lord paramount, and the result is melancholy. Ruined, insulted, and disappointed, the Servians can hardly be restrained from openly declaring against us. The Servians were promised Constantinople, and now have to beg for the restitution of their former territory."

The *St. Petersburg Exchange Gazette* says:—

"It would require the pen of a Plutarch to clothe in suitable words the following telegram just received from Semlin:—'In the battle of Djunis the Servians lost 1,500 men, the Russians 2,500. All these were killed. There are hardly any wounded.' This is astounding news. The Russians, who form but a small portion of the Servian army, lose 2,500, and these are killed; the Servians, on the other hand, register only 1,500. Whose was the accursed, the sacrilegious hand, O ye deceased heroes! that exposed you to the destructive fire of the enemy, until nearly every one of you had been destroyed? Who dared to throw away your valour, to waste your manhood? The question is a terrible one, but one that should be answered frankly and fully. From a telegram in the *Moscow Gazette* we learn that the artillery mutinied at Djunis; that the men refused to take orders from General Tchernaieff, and quitted the field without firing a shot. Hence we are driven to the conclusion that though the artillery refused to share in the battle, the Commander-in-Chief left the small handful of his countrymen to bear the onslaught of a large hostile force. The Servians forsaking him, he had no compunction in sacrificing the Russians, who, he knew, would prefer death to flight. The ambitious gambler staked the lives of several thousands of his countrymen upon his last card, and lost his stake. If there is any other explanation to be offered, for God's sake let us hear it. Though the time for settling accounts with M. Tchernaieff has hardly come, we and other newspaper editors have to confess a certain complicity in his career. We have to own to withholding from our readers a great deal of the intelligence that reached us from the Morava Army. We thought it wrong to weaken M. Tchernaieff's authority when money was being collected for volunteers fighting under his orders. Now, when M. Tchernaieff is no longer wanted in Servia, and other officers will lead the Russian troops against the Turks, we are free to say that the news which has reached us from time to time is by no means wholly favourable to him."

After some further severe strictures of Tchernaieff for his lying and other faults, the article concludes:—

"As a fitting climax the Servian army has been destroyed, and a whole detachment of Russian volunteers sacrificed to the ambition of their Commander-in-Chief. We have no wish to injure M. Tchernaieff—we are, on the contrary, ready to believe that he meant well; but we think it necessary to say that he has shown himself altogether unfit for the great task undertaken by him. As war may be in store for us, idols should be abolished."

The Russian officers who went to Servia were quite worthy of the cause in which they were engaged. Professor Viskowatoff, who accompanied a hospital train to the seat of war, relates as follows:—

"I had scarcely landed at Belgrade when I was startled by a Russian officer reeling along the street intoxicated. He had come to fight for an idea; and he was now heard clamouring for spirits and insulting the passers-by. All attempts to quiet him he answered by invectives and a threatening display of his sword. At last there was nothing to be done but to throw him down, bind him, and carry him to the hotel. . . . Unfortunately, a good many Russians have made their way to Servia, not to fight, but to drink for the idea of liberty. It is quite intelligible that the Servians are not particularly edified by the manners and customs of these strangers, who, to crown all, claim to be regarded as their saviours. The Servians are a quiet and reserved race, little inclined to tippling; the Russian is noisy, gesticulates, and likes a dram." *

We close here with a sense of relief our sketch of the Bulgarian and other atrocities,† as well as the first attempt of the Panslavists to take Constantinople by surprise. What the next scene in the tragedy will be remains to be seen. The first miserable act has been played out, and its hero, Tchernaieff, consigned to limbo.

---

* Those extracts are taken principally from the *Times*, Nov. 5, 1876.

† See the Black Book of Russia for further particulars.

BOOK III.

THE SOLUTION OF
THE EASTERN QUESTION.

BOOK III.

CHAPTER I.

THE SOLUTION OF THE EASTERN QUESTION.

What is meant by a solution of the Eastern Question? We may say of the solution as we did of the definition of the Eastern Question. If one were to visit all the *salons* where diplomatists do congregate, from Vienna to London, he would hear everywhere that the Eastern Question is not ripe for solution. The same phrase runs through the Blue Books and newspapers. But it would be much nearer the truth if we were to say that up to the present time our statesmen have not had the courage to look the matter in the face, and say how it must be solved. For, indeed, there is only one solution of the matter possible, and that has been foreshadowed in the order of Divine Providence, who has higher and more distinguished considerations in view than those usually falling to the lot of Embassies.

Not ripe for solution! is the exclamation of the timid, who are afraid of the consequences of solving it; or it may be the ignorant, who do not know what there is to solve. It is no use disguising the matter at all. The Eastern Question has to be solved in blood. It is simply a series of surgical operations, which will have to be performed with more or less skill, and the final question is which of the parties upon whom the amputations are to be performed can best endure the depletion. There are three, Russia, Austria, and Turkey who *must* go into the operating room; others, especially England, may be dragged in, but for the three former there is no escape.

For many years past Russia has been, like one of the magicians which we read of in the books of the Occult Brethren, who "call spirits from the vasty deep," with this shade of difference, that they called those they could master and allay. She, by her greed, rapacity, and brutal lusts, has awakened demons which she is quite unable to control. They have taken possession of her body and soul, and they are all imps of blood. The Panslavists would lead her to battle in a hoped for conquest of Turkey and Austria. The Nihilists are waiting quietly at home, praying that the armed legions which are sent forth may be swept into the Danube, and then the Commune will be proclaimed under the Red Flag.

The very first thing, then, to be determined in the solution of the Eastern question is, WHAT IS RUSSIA'S PLACE IN THE FAMILY OF EUROPEAN NATIONS? It cannot be what it has been in the past, it cannot remain what it is in the present; that is as impossible as it would be to arrest the advancing decrepitude of age, or for the body to live in a state of perpetual fever. For in reality there are three Russias, but the bands that bind them together are by no means strong, and even those are being consumed with burning hate. First of all there is Imperial Russia, of which the Emperor is the head. This might almost be termed Germanic Russia; but its power is very great, holding, as it does, fifty per cent. of the offices of the State; being also the most gifted and highly trained, it maintains its position by sheer intellectual force. It looks down upon the fierce Russ, the Slav, the Cossack, and Calmuck as beings of an inferior order, born to till the earth, gather in the harvests, breed the cattle, and be drilled into a human machine, which shall fight with the pitilessness of death whenever it is required.

The contempt of the German is repaid by the hatred of the Slav. The Slav feels his inferiority in his inmost soul, but with his tongue he utters a boasting that never escapes from the lips of his

Teutonic master. How little sympathy there is between those two classes may be perceived by the fact that the German colonists, who were induced to settle in Russia by Catherine II. more than a century ago, have never mixed in the least with the Russians around them, and they remain there now, free from taxation, as disdainful of their neighbours, and as much objects of aversion to them as they were at the time of the great Empress.

By the Slav or Panslav party, we must not speak as though it included the great mass of that race. The leading element of it may be called the Slav, which is a Russo-Slav, in the same sense as we employ the term Anglo-Saxon. It is this element which gives courage, daring, and force to the Imperial army; it is, indeed, the military energy of the nation that intends to cut out of the map of Europe with its keen and pitiless sword the great Panslavonic Empire shown on our map. This party regards the Empress as its head, and the Cesarevitch as its future leader; General Ignatieff director of the Panslavonic committee of Moscow and its representative at Constantinople; Kauffmann, the conqueror of Khiva, its highest military commander, and Tchernaieff its "filibustering" adventurer. It is, in reality, the only potent and dangerous element which Western Europe has to dread in Russia.

But great Russia, or, as it has been called, "Free Russia," has little thought, or feeling, or sympathy with either of the above parties. What was serf Russia has been set free from its former masters. It has gained its emancipation from the noble and is handed over to the tax collector and drill-sergeant. The landed nobility have lost their interest in the serfs and are irreconcilably offended with the Emperor and his party for giving them their liberty; while the serf on his part feels bitterly aggrieved that his freedom has brought him so little.

The terms of his emancipation were considered liberal by most statesmen; to him this liberality was a delusion and a snare. It increased his burden of life and took from him his protector, in whom he had formerly trusted.

The lot of the peasant is hard indeed. Before he has arrived at the age of manhood he is taken from his home to be drilled into a soldier, for the conscription is universal. He must leave all he loves behind him and serve at least for six years in the army. This six, however, may be prolonged to twenty, and indeed is in the case of some hundreds of thousands of men. Their pay is small, their food coarse, the drill severe, the barrack accommodation often wretched. This is bad for those who are taken from their homes: those who remain there find life equally bitter. Their toil is incessant during the short summer months. They wrestle with a poor soil, and draw from it but scanty crops, which are rendered less by their want of capital and skill as agriculturists. Indeed, owing to this latter fact, the soil which formerly sent so much corn to the English market is now pretty well exhausted. There have been several bad harvests in succession, not from the inclemency of the elements, but simply from the want of skill in those who have the management of the soil. The poor peasant and farmer have therefore but little to spare. Southern Russia, that formerly supplied us with so much wheat from Odessa, Azov, and Taganrog, do not send half their usual quantity, and very soon this outlet for their industry will be a thing of the past. The people have, therefore, but little to sell for which money in any form can be obtained. The burden of the wretched paper money falls also upon their shoulders, and, to crown all, if after his incessant toil and struggle the poor fellow has a copec in his pocket, the tax-collector comes and takes it from him with the knout.

There has been little time, even if there had been desire and opportunity, for the education of the serf, for it is not long since his emancipation was decreed; but there is a more powerful reason than this for his ignorance. There is no money to provide schools, nor teachers to conduct them if they were built; nor, indeed, time, except in winter, for the pupils to attend. Only three per cent. of the whole population of Russia can read and write.

But although they have no schoolmasters, they

have teachers among them. The Nihilists and the missionaries of the "Old Believers," pass from one smoky crib to another, and whisper the secrets of their faith to ears greedy to devour them. They tell them that their emancipation is a fraud; only one, however, among a number of swindles equally cunning and gigantic. They have been swindled out of the very earth they tread upon. Is not the land theirs? Did not their fathers re-claim it from the bog and the wilderness, and did the prince, noble, or priest lend a hand to them while doing it? and do not their hands and stalwart muscles hold it from going back again to the wolf, the bear, and the stork?

And they hold it on condition of paying rent and taxes with money. And the money itself is the greatest swindle of all. The gold, platina, silver and copper coins, are all the Emperor's. They have his image stamped upon them. Very little of it is allowed to pass through their hands, but the metal becomes a chain of slavery. They cannot do without it, and they cannot hold it. It is simply a scourge, that takes the last energy out of their exhausted limbs. They hold it during one brief night's sleep, to wake with renewed energy, to toil again for the possession of that which is taken from them immediately it is earned.

And the Nihilist tells them that the money swindle does not end there. The honest metal, if they could only keep or use it, might be tolerated. It is, however, only the basis of a superstructure of paper-money and credit, which multiplies the evil by millions. The peasant is told that he works the first fresh hours of the day for the Emperor's coin; toils on through mid-day far into the afternoon for the shadow of the coin, which he gets in the form of paper-money, upon which a race of vampires, capitalists, bankers, and others who trade in money, realise immense fortunes, all reaped from the sweat of his face.* Then come the middle man and merchant, who take their profits out of his labour. In the evening, if exhausted nature will bear it, he may work an hour for himself, and share the result of his toil with the priest. His emancipation has **only** completed this great swindle of peasant life.

This is only a condensed report of a portion of a speech of the Russian representative of the Secret Societies, delivered at the International Convention at Geneva, and was received with applause by the majority of those present.

Russia is, therefore, the land of hatreds; of mistrusts, of brutal force, and abject cowardice; of profuse waste in some parts of the public service, of galling wretchedness in others. The nobles mistrust the Emperor; the Emperor and his party dread

---

* The money-lenders in Russia are called *miroiedy*-eaters of the Mir—the community, or world. The peasant pays 100 per cent. for a loan. See *Revue des Deux Mondes*, 15th Nov., 1876, p. 270.

the Panslavists, who in their turn hate the Germans and despise those who do not embrace their cause; while the peasants hate, with little discrimination, except the Emperor, all above them. Their devotion to His Majesty savours of idolatry, but their love and admiration extend little beyond him. They hate the nobility, who may have been cruel to them in past times, and who possess the best of the land at present. The war department, that takes away their finest young men — Jews, bankers, money dealers in general; and what is phenomenal, and not, I believe, to be found elsewhere, although devout, they have the most thorough detestation of their priests, whom they at present spit at and curse, but who are reserved for something worse when the new age is proclaimed.

Russia is strong, then, in the number of her soldiers, the excellence of their discipline, and in the undoubted courage and daring of a portion of them; and to this must be added the pangs of hunger and the recklessness of despair. The conviction has sunk into the pale, wan heart of Russia that she cannot be worse, and although the Emperor and his party, to some extent, guide and curb the military passion, and keep the peasantry in subjection, this cannot last long; the bloodhounds will slip the collar sooner or later, and then will the cry of "havoc" arise.

Such is Russia's strength: let us now glance at her

weakness. It is useless to disguise the fact that if the plan of a Panslavonic Empire could be carried out, the finer forms of European civilisation must perish. Even the attempt to realise it must involve a gigantic war of many years' duration.

The prime cause of Russia's weakness lies in the innermost core of the Slav heart. It is void of truth, and this want of veracity spreads its rottenness into every department of the State. The Emperor's plighted word is worthless; the despatches of his Ministers and Ambassadors bundles of chaff; the Civil Service of the State is administered in a form coarse, brutal, and corrupt. Even the army is, to a large extent, a sham: 1,250,000 men look overwhelmingly formidable on paper, but so rotten is the commissariat and supply department that it can hardly move, much less be kept in motion. It is a huge animal, like some of the megalosaurus of the reptile age; but it cannot run, since its legs, always weak, are now eaten out with disease. And the navy is no better; nay, it is said to be even worse than the army, and the Russian war-fleet no more dare encounter that of Turkey than a carrion crow can do battle with a falcon. Russia is very prudent in the use of her ships of war. She took her last Black Sea fleet into Sebastopol and sunk it, evidently thinking the bottom of the sea the proper place for it.

We referred in a former chapter to the expensive

but utterly useless conquests of Russia in Central Asia. But few people have an idea of the immense extent of country which they have acquired in that region. It comprises altogether over 325,000 square miles, an area as large as Germany and Italy put together, and in the whole of this vast territory the population does not exceed 1,600,000 souls. Of those, more than one-half are nomads, wandering over the plains and subsisting on their flocks and herds, so that the settled population is little more than that of a first-class English town, and the whole not half the population of London.

It may be very well asked, why conquer and hold such a useless possession? And the reason is not far to seek. The conquerors received high rewards and honours, and the administration, civil and military, affords an opportunity for many posts, in which, although the salary may be small, the peculations are enormous. Boards and offices are created which have no duties to perform. There is a forest department, where there are not a score of trees in the whole district; a mining department without mines, and 22,000 roubles a year is given for the support of the *Turkistan Gazette*. The result is, that in 1872, the last years for which I have any returns, the total income was 2,008,374 roubles, the expenditure 7,576,116 roubles, thus leaving a deficiency of 5,567,842 roubles.

It is not necessary to pursue this subject, or it

would be easy to trace out the extravagance, peculation, and depravity which pervades the whole of the administration. A high Russian authority, cited by Mr. Schuyler, thus accounts for the breakdown of their system of government:—

"The most of the functionaries of our adminstration in Central Asia have been distinguished by their bad characters. They have wasted the money of the Crown on their own pleasures; and, notwithstanding that several of them have been pardoned, while their inferiors have been condemned, the investigations, which the Government ordered to discover the guilty parties, lingered on for several years and remained without result. The natives see all these regrettable facts, and comment on them in their manner. They say, 'How are the Russians better than the Khokandians? They also take away our daughters and our wives, and also love presents; and waste the money of the Tsar as the Beks wasted that of the Khans.'"

He further adds:—"Everybody thinks only of making a quick career; of occupying an advantageous post and of obtaining increased rank; and nobody gives himself the trouble to take into account the duties imposed upon him by the fact of his being Russian."

Occasionally we get a view at the doings of these gentlemen. There was, for instance, at Tashkent, a drunken soldier who wore a civil dress, kept a private lodging-house, a carpenter's shop, and a drinking-house. This individual took part payment from fully twenty persons, under the pretext of guaranteeing, by the money he received, a contract for wood which he had with the Government and deceived them all, for he neither performed his promise nor repaid the advances.

Illegal taxes are by no means uncommon. Thus we are told* that the Prefect of the district of Kurama levied 90,000 roubles of illegal taxes in one year, and spent the whole of it for his own use. He was punished by being removed to a more lucrative post.

We have cases also recorded of people being subjected to torture, sometimes for the purpose of extorting money from them or to frighten them against giving evidence of the peculations of the Russians. Indeed, force, fraud, peculation, and torture are the characteristics of the Russian Government throughout her Asiatic possessions.

The possessions of Russia in Central Asia are not only unprofitable at present, but they have become an expensive luxury, such as a rich nation, even like England could not afford to maintain, much less a people so poor and oppressed as those under the dominion of the Czar. It may interest those who have been lending their money so freely to Russia to know that the golden stream that flows from their pockets is spent mostly in unremunerative works,

* See Schuyler, Vol. II., p. 247.

and that many of the streams are like the rivers of Central Asia and Africa, absorbed in desert sands. There is no country in the world where corruption is so universal, and jobbery so common. Not even the United States of America, with its whiskey rings and other adroit schemes for fleecing Uncle Sam, can compare with Holy Russia. It is rotten to the heart's core; there is a lie upon every tongue, and a swindled copec in every pocket.

As an example of the manner in which public works are carried out in Russia, one undertaking will pretty well illustrate all the rest. We heard much, some years ago, about the great works which Russia was about to undertake on the Sea of Aral, and how the Syr-Darya was to be made navigable. Now, all who know anything about those regions—and none are better acquainted with the facts than the Russians themselves—are aware that any improvements of the kind are impossible. For centuries past, indeed, for countless ages, there has been a gradual up-heaving of the earth's crust in Central Asia, extending over many thousands of square miles, emptying vast lakes or inland seas, causing mighty rivers to disappear altogether, and in this way changing the whole surface of the country. The waters of the Caspian are disappearing at the rate of one foot in a century, and as for the Aral it is already so shallow that for all purposes of navigation it is comparatively speaking worthless. More than this, the receding waters have left its shores in almost every direction, utterly worthless. They are barren wastes of sand or salt, except where the rivers debouch into the lake, and there are still more fatal morasses. And it was in those unprofitable regions that Russian speculation and peculation found its legitimate sphere.

The first attempt to render the Syr-Darya navigable was made in 1853. Large embankments were built, which were swept away by the next rainy season. The dykes were again rebuilt in the following autumn and winter, and were again swept away, as everybody knew they would be. In 1856 Lieut. Butakof attempted to widen a small stream connecting the Kara-Uziak with the Jamau-Darya, in hope of avoiding the navigation of the very narrowest part of the river and straightening the channel. These works were continued with vigour during the next two years, but had to be given up as the water did not rise high enough to wash away the barriers in the manner he proposed. In the year 1860 an attempt was made to clean out the channel of the Kara-Uziak for a distance of four miles, and after working on it for nearly two years it was abandoned as an utterly useless proceeding. A similar attempt was made in 1862, with the same result. In 1864 a new exploration was made of the river, and Captain Schott reported that it would be easy to clean out the bed and render it navigable. A second expedition, however, reported that this would be impossible. It was then resolved to dig a canal from the Syr-Darya to the Jaman-Darya. On the 21st of June the canal was opened, and it was believed that the high waters of the following spring would widen it and render it navigable for ships. On the contrary, the canal was filled up with sand, and the navigation made worse than ever. Since that time the whole of the works have been abandoned.

Finding digging an unprofitable affair, or, indeed, that the farce could be kept up no longer, it was resolved to try navigation, and henceforth a fleet for the Aral formed one of the items of Muscovite news. It is true, there were no places to trade at or people to trade with upon the coast; still, two schooners were built and launched—one for surveying, the other for fishing, purposes. But as neither of them dared go out to sea, this ended like the canal-cutting. Then steamers were tried. Some were built in Sweden, others in England; but, having their steamers, the difficulty was to get fuel for them. The *saksaul* was dear, and the supply limited, and the coal distant and expensive. Besides this, the shallow waters, by bringing the bottom of the vessel in constant contact with the sand, soon wore out the iron plates of the ships. Large pontoons were then tried, but proved utterly unmanageable. Then barges were attempted, and, after all, it was discovered that the goods intended to be carried across the lakes in vessels could be transported along its shores on camels as cheap, and much more safely. We ought not, perhaps, to omit to add that one of the vessels was armed with a due complement of guns, though there was no foe or any fort to shoot at.

The grand result, then, of all this outlay, which must in its totality considerably exceed a million of money, borrowed from the credulous English, is, that there is one poor steamer at present upon the Aral, namely, the "Samarkand," which was purchased in Belgium for 78,700 roubles, and that the amount of "private" freight which it carried the last year for which we have any return, viz., 1869, was twenty-four tons. So much for the promotion of commercial enterprise in Central Asia.[*]

The solution, then, or rather the dissolution, of Russia, is the real EASTERN QUESTION. It was she who proposed it, and, properly interpreted for Western Europe, it is rather a Northern than an Eastern question. Russia comes from the North to the South to conquer, to kill, to steal. There have been wars in which the conqueror had something to bestow upon the conquered. Such were our wars in India. We put down princes, but we offered the people better laws, better administration, lighter taxes, facilities and capital for the development of the resources of their country; and if a

---

[*] See Schuyler's "Turkestan," Vol. II., p. 56.

foe dared threaten, then the British sword flashed in his face. We are giving them also science, art, literature, intellectual culture, universities, colleges, schools, and freedom, their personal liberty and right to their own form of worship.

But what has Russia to give? She has borrowed her reigning and governing class from Germany; her diplomatic language from France; her mechanical skill, the little she possesses, from England; her capital from wherever she could borrow it; and as for her credit, like Falstaff, she has used it so "damnably" that it will last no longer.

The map of the proposed Panslavonic Empire shows the limits at which she is willing to solve the Eastern Question for the present, and in exchange for those fertile provinces and the subjugation of so many millions of people, she has one thing, and one only, to offer—THE KNOUT.

CHAPTER II.

CAN THE EASTERN QUESTION BE SOLVED BY REFORMS DEMANDED OF TURKEY?

WE have seen in the preceding Book how the net has been gradually drawn around Turkey by the three Powers, who were bent on her spoliation. The Secret Societies had invaded her territories. The Austrian Consul at Ragusa supplied them with arms, and Sir H. Elliot early in February, 1876, wrote to Lord Derby, to inform him of what was taking place at Constantinople. He says: "The Russian Consulate is the open resort of the insurgent chiefs; their correspondence is sent to the Consul, who is a party to all their projects, and associates himself intimately with them." Servia and Montenegro were preparing openly to take the field, the slow process of bleeding to death not having had the desired effect; and in this turmoil of affairs, and a future overhung with black clouds surcharged with blood, Turkey is called upon to not only grant reforms, but to give guarantees for their being carried out in perpetuity.

Now there was, and, indeed, still is, an immense convenience in urging these reforms upon Turkey. Independent of any merit that may be in them the parties proposing the schemes fully intend that they never shall be accepted. The primary condition, indeed, in all of them was, that they should be one of three things—either

Such as Turkey could not accept without giving up her sovereignty over the European provinces, and leaving the Moslems at the mercy of their enemies; or,

Such as Austria might propose and Russia object to; or,

Such as Austria and Russia might approve of, and the *Secret Societies* disdain.

Under these conditions it is scarcely necessary to discuss what those proposed reforms really were. So far as Austria and Russia were concerned, they were got up on purpose for exportation, and fully realise the ancient fable of the wolf preaching to the lamb, or the butcher warning the sheep to restrain his carnivorous propensities. Still, REFORM is a good word, and has a magic sound in it, especially for the people of England, France, and Germany, and hence was held up as a banner, under which Emperors could mature their schemes of aggrandisement; Secret Societies ripen their plots; and conspirators, brigands, jail-birds, and gipsies, dabble their hands in innocent blood.

We, in England, happen to know something of reforms, and how difficult it is to attain them under the best and most favourable circumstances. It usually takes a generation to effect any great change in our social life: it took more than this to bring about Catholic emancipation; fully as long to convert the nation from protection to the wise and enlightened doctrines of free trade; it took an equal length of time to procure an extension of the suffrage to its present broad basis; and what shall we say of our education? It is nearly two centuries ago since Wase, who was the first to propose the education of *the whole people,* issued his celebrated book. A century later, others began to talk about it; and early in the present century Bell and Lancaster showed how the work could be accomplished; and now, half a century after Lancaster commenced his school, the nation has entered resolutely upon the work. But it is not yet accomplished, and hence the dense ignorance of great masses of our people.

But supposing any of those great works had been attempted when a rebellion was raging in Ireland, with the avowed object of driving the English into the sea, if no opportunity occurred of cutting their throats before they got there; that an armada of iron-clads was waiting at Cherbourg, and Kauffmann with his orthodox army waiting to embark at Calais; and

Scotland had declared war, and was about to invade Northumberland, could those reforms even have been talked about, much less accomplished?

And yet this is precisely what Turkey is called upon to do. She has to pass a measure, or proclaim a law, far more sweeping than our Catholic Emancipation Act; to introduce a system of judicial reform more extensive than that which has been accomplished in England from the days of James I. to our latest Judicature Act; and to revise her mode of taxation, and bring about changes in her financial affairs equal to those which we have been able to effect in England since Cromwell first substituted indirect for direct taxation.

And the demand that she shall do all this is made at a time when Russia has hold of one arm, Austria of the other, Montenegro and Servia are plunging daggers into her feet, and the Secret Societies hold a sword at her throat.

The difficulty of introducing reforms into Turkey is again increased and complicated by the vested interests which foreigners have acquired in the administration of her affairs. We have heard a great deal of late about the right that the Great Powers have obtained by the Treaty of 1856, for the protection of the Christians in European Turkey. But this is a small matter in comparison with other rights and privileges which foreign nations have acquired in Turkey. It is a singular thing that those difficulties have arisen out of pure good nature and indifference on the part of the Turk.

Three centuries ago some of the Italian States obtained a right to trade with Turkey, and those rights were confirmed and regulated by firmans, which are known in history as "capitulations;" and it was under one of those arrangements that in 1595 the English were allowed to trade with Turkey.

The conditions granted to our countrymen by Mohammed IV. confirmed and extended the arrangements which had been previously granted, and gave protection to our merchants who ventured on the perilous field of Turkish commerce. How perilous that field was then esteemed to be may be judged from the fact that the Ironmongers' Company still have a legacy, amounting to over four thousand a year, which was left at that time for the redemption of captives in Barbary.

What the Sultan did, therefore, was a beneficent act. Article 19 of the Capitulation says: "If the corsairs' or galliots of the Levant shall be found to have taken any English vessels, or robbed or plundered them of their goods and effects, also, if anyone shall have forcibly taken anything from the English, all possible diligence and exertion shall be used and employed for the discovery of the property, and inflicting condign punishment on those who may have committed such depredations, and their ships, goods, and effects shall be restored to them without delay or intrigue."*

These capitulations are distinctly stated to have been granted through friendship and as a special imperial favour to the King of England, who was allowed "with His own money to purchase for his own kitchen, at Smyrna, Salonica, or any other port in our sacred dominion, in fertile and abundant years, and not in times of dearth or scarcity, two cargoes of figs and raisins."

It was also further granted that Embassies might be established at such ports as should be agreed upon by Article 45, and that no English subject should be reproved, beaten, or put in prison without the consent of our Ambassador.

From this grant spring up what are known in the East as "Consular Courts." Foreigners were not only exempt from all taxation, but could only be tried by their own countrymen. "In no other country in the world, having equal rank as a State," says Mr. Farley, "do foreigners hold such a privileged position as in Turkey. For example, they are exempt from all imposts whatsoever, either State or municipal, customs' dues alone excepted. They may lead a life of pleasure or of business, may settle and amass wealth, or may travel and spend it; and at all times may claim the fullest protection which the laws of the Empire are capable of affording, without

---

* See Harslet, II., p. 350. See also Farley's "Modern Turkey."

contributing one piastre to the expenses of the State, and without being amenable in the smallest degree to Ottoman jurisdiction. If the Porte construct a road, light a town with gas, or pave and cleanse a street, it cannot compel the foreign residents to contribute a para towards the cost, while the whole system of taxation is rendered irregular and difficult in consequence of the mischievous obstructions offered by these charters in nearly every relation between the foreign population and the Government."

We have lately also heard much about the mal-administration of the law in Turkey, but few people are aware that the principal difficulties arise as much from the power given to foreigners by those "capitulations" as from any inherent defects in the native courts. For instance, an Englishman is altogether independent of the civil and criminal law of the country, and can only be judged by his own Consul, and in accordance with English, not Turkish law. Another abuse has grown out of this strange privilege. A number of natives—most of them not "righteous over much"—have managed by one means and another to obtain foreign passports, or naturalisation, and thus relieve themselves from Ottoman authority. If one of those "protected foreigners" commits a murder he cannot be arrested without the consent of his own Consul, and if the villain be hotly pursued, and takes refuge in the house of some one of another nationality, that house cannot be entered without the presence of a delegate from that foreigner's Consulate.

In the recovery of a debt the matter would be more complicated and absurd. Anyone having a claim against a foreigner must prosecute it before the Consul or Consulate Judge of the nation, to which the defendant belongs, and as there are sixteen different Consulates in Turkey, he may be obliged to sue in as many different courts, supposing that one person of each nation owes him a debt. This is an anomaly to all our international law and usage; even in Russia and Greece there is no such jurisdiction.

But every Consul in Turkey is ready to fight tooth and nail for this privilege, and among other things it has been demanded that foreigners may be able to hold land in that country, which, like their personal property, shall be exempt from the tithes and taxation. A modest demand, surely.

That legal reforms are greatly needed in Turkey is perfectly true, but scarcely more than they are in Russia, and many other countries. It is not long ago that one of the principal citizens of Odessa was taken from his home, and carried right off to Siberia without trial of any kind; neither has his offence, if he committed any, been made public to this very day. Even in America we learn it is not an uncommon thing for judges to be bribed; but who believes the Americans are going to let their judicial system remain unreformed, or that they could or would attempt to make any great changes with a rebellion raging in two States, and armed foreign intervention threatened? "You can't swop horses while crossing a river," said President Lincoln.

The finances of Turkey are in a bad state, but so far as the collection of the taxes is concerned the Greek Christians have no more cause of complaint than the Latins, Jews, or even the Mussulmans. The manner in which the country is taxed is a just and proper one, since it is a tax upon the wealth produced, which, out of its surplus, does, and ought to, maintain the Government. It is simply in the method of collecting, which costs about fifty per cent. instead of ten, where the abuses creep in. The taxes are what is called farmed. A speculator pays to, or guarantees the Government, the whole tax for a certain district, and having made his bargain and paid a certain sum in advance, he divides and sub-divides his purchase into smaller lots, out of which every purchaser realises a profit; hence that which the State sells for fifty not unfrequently produces a hundred pounds. Of the tax itself, and the reform that should be adopted in its collection, Mr. Barron, in his official report, says:—

"The tithe is the only practicable land tax in a country like Turkey. It is, moreover, recognised by the religion of Islam, and, combined with the sheep tax, itself a kind of tithe, was the only tax regularly

Q

enforced in the Arab and Turkish Empires. To remove all the abuses attendant on this or any other tax would be impossible. The object of a statesman should be to reconcile together the dictates of equity, the interests of the Treasury, and the national habits. On this principle the best expedient would seem to be an extensive application of the system of compounding for tithes. The system might be applied to whole "kazes," to communes, and even to single farms, either for one or several years in advance, and by a free consent of both parties."

We have reason to know that this system will, so soon as possible, be adopted by the Turkish Government, and it will, perhaps, surprise some of our readers to be informed that, bad as the method of collecting the Turkish revenue is, the Empire is more lightly taxed than Russia, Austria, Germany, or France.

Still Turkey is summoned, at the cannon's mouth, to reform the method of collecting her revenue; and by Russia, too, who knouts a man to death if he does not yield up his last copec to the tax-gatherer.

While speaking upon this question of Turkish Reform, it may not be amiss to say something about the phrase so commonly used by Russia and her friends—AUTONOMY, and what is meant by an autonomy of the Christian provinces.

Although the Russians are very careful not to

define what autonomy means in their vocabulary, still the thing creeps out in their suggestions and in the utterances of the Panslavonic agitators. The absolute meaning of the word is SELF-ACTING, and hence, when Lord Derby uses the phrase "autonomous administration," he is very nearly using the English term for "local self-government." But all English phrases and institutions have to be modified before they can be adopted or even understood in the East, and hence it means one thing on the banks of the Danube and another on the Thames.

So far as the claims of Russia are concerned it would be much better to use the noun instead of the verb, and call the thing an automaton, "an image moved by springs." The church and schools in Bulgaria are autonomous, with every priest and schoolmaster a traitor to Turkey, and a member in virtue of his office of the Panslavonic Association. Autonomy, then, when used by those gentlemen, means that the State should follow the example of the church and school and become Russianised —a machine of which the Czar kept the key.

Hence, whenever reforms are mentioned in reference to Turkey we always hear the word "guarantee;" and this word, again, means one thing with most English people, and another with the Russians. With us it means a treaty, or solemn undertaking to do certain things which have been specified and agreed upon as desirable. It is, indeed, a covenant which all the parties to it are bound to observe. The Panslavists, however, mean something widely different from this. They mean some Turkish provinces which they may be allowed to occupy with an armed force, without war, that they may disarm the Turks, arm the Christians, and in this way cast Islam out of Europe. As the Americans would say, "improve the Moslems off the face of the earth." In his inmost soul the Slav fears the Turk, and hence wants to cross the Danube under European protection.

Well, the Mussulmans say, Not a foot of our territory must be yielded to anyone, much less to Russia. We are glad of the friendship of England, and receive with open arms her teachers of science and art, her skilled artisans and mechanics; and we offer in return a rich field for the investment of her enterprise and wealth. We esteem, also, the genius, culture, and enterprise of France; and the deep thought and learning of Germany. But Russia has nothing to give us—neither science, art, literature, learning, money, or goods. She comes, hungry as one of her own Polar bears in mid-winter, to eat up our rich inheritance, and has nothing to give us in return but the edge of the sword, or, at best, the knout.

But "what are reforms on paper?" it is inquired. If the reader will go into the British Museum he may be able to answer that question satisfactorily.

There is in the King's Library the Great Charter signed by King John. It is only a piece of vellum, but it is the foundation of England's liberties.

The Hatti-Hum-oivod, then, is the Magna Charta of Turkish liberty. Like ours, it was first of all only a piece of parchment with certain thoughts and laws written upon it. Gradually, for life is of slow growth, the national life is transformed to that ideal, and the result is—a free people.

But where is the charter of Russia's liberty? Behold! it is written in the knout, and the free use of that is unrestricted!

The Eastern Question, then, cannot be solved in Turkey; because, if the Turks were driven out of Europe the question would still be, who shall command the Danube? above all who shall hold Constantinople?

CHAPTER III.

REFORMS DEMANDED BY THE SECRET SOCIETIES.

NEVER since the " Old Man of the Mountain " held the world in terror has there been, that I am aware of, such a state of things as exists at present in Eastern Europe. An organisation, not only secret, but, so far as its known leaders are concerned, impalpable, or at least intangible, has taken its place at the council boards of empires and assumed the dictatorship.

It is not necessary for us to trace either the origin or development of those societies. They were at first derided, then persecuted, now feared, so that neither Austria nor Russia dare lift a finger against them. Cabinet ministers, generals in the army, bishops and ministers of religion, merchants, capitalists have thrown in their lot with them. The miserable in all places; the wicked, wherever they have an opportunity, combine to form the phalanx. They have power in the state, the press, the church, on the exchanges of Europe; they have their armies in some places, and the assassin's knife everywhere.

Another characteristic of those secret organisations is that, so far as they themselves are concerned, they have abolished morality, and we might add religion also, only that some of their ideas carry us into extreme Socialism. We have, therefore, to deal with an entirely new element in the political potencies of the world.

There is a curious, and, but for its tragical consequences, an amusing phase in this alliance of crowned heads and secret conspirators. The Emperors of Russia and Austria did not call those spirits from the vasty deep; they had risen spontaneously from the nether regions, and came uninvited into their councils, where they were, however, welcomed as allies. Each believed, and in reality did, as the boys say, take each other in. The Empires are like the two giants, who are said in the Talmud to have got astride of the ark until the flood became impatient of the super-imposed burden, and threw them over to sink into the mud of a lost world. It is thus that the Secret Societies, according to their own estimation, allow the giants to float on upon the rippling surface of their murky waters. When the proper time comes they will be plunged into what the Zendavesta calls Duzgah's depths, to be purified as best may be in the everlasting fire.

When Count Andrassy therefore came upon the

stage, like the clown turned gravedigger in "Hamlet," he occupied the audience with his quips and quirks, while the power behind the curtain matured its programme. Time, however, was required by those sons of Belial, and hence the three Powers set themselves to concoct the Berlin Memorandum, which, like the Andrassy Note, came to what it was worth—nothing!

The grand object however of the Insurgents had been obtained; time had been gained, and the action of the Turkish forces paralysed. The demands now put forward are somewhat singular. Instead of praying to be saved from the just doom of traitors and assassins—which, if mortal men ever merited, they richly deserve—they put in claims such as few conquerors ever yet proposed to a subjugated people.

The reader must bear in mind that the region of which they are speaking is a desolate and howling wilderness, and made so by them; that the country, always stony and rough, with a few bright cultivated spots, where cosy villages nestled among the trees, and sheltered by the protecting rocks around them, had been thoroughly ravaged and laid desolate. The Christians with their flocks and herds had been removed, and their houses burnt and razed to the ground. The Turks had been butchered, their houses destroyed, their cattle and property stolen, and it was this province which the insurgents call a "State," to which their demands refer. They demanded in the first place one-third of the landed property of the Turks. Next, that the Turkish troops should be withdrawn, with the exception of certain small garrisons which could be butchered when convenient. Third, that Turkey should cause to be rebuilt the houses and churches which they, the insurgents, had burnt, and shall provide food for the Christians for at least a year, also seed and agricultural implements, and exempt them from taxation for three years.

Fourth, that the Christians should retain their arms, and the Mussulmans surrender theirs, while the reforms are in process of execution.

That the leaders of the insurrection should assemble and determine how far those changes should extend to other provinces of the Turkish Empire, such as Bosnia for instance.

Sixth. Since *the insurgents cannot trust to the simple promises of the Porte*, they desire to nominate a treasurer of their own to take charge of the funds necessary for the re-building of towns, churches, store-houses, and other convenient places.

Finally, they demand that all the garrisons occupied by Turkish troops shall be under the control of Austrian and Russian agents.

They modestly conclude, "*while we dare not ask for more*, we cannot on the other hand ask for less."

The whole of this precious document is given in "Affairs of Turkey," No. III., p. 84 and 85.

Our Consul, Mr. Holmes, makes an interesting calculation as to the amount of money that the Turk would have had to put at the disposal of the insurgent "treasurer." The cost of re-building the houses was estimated at something over a million, and upon the subject of the maintenance of the returning refugees, Mr. Monson, writing to Lord Derby, says:—

"Mr. Holmes writes to me that at Mostar the expense of maintaining for fourteen months the returned refugees and the rest of the inhabitants of the Herzegovina is calculated at £2,000,000 Turkish. But Danetsch Effendi, the Turkish Consul-General here, says that this is an excessive estimate, and that the calculation he made here with Vassi Effendi is as follows:—'300,000 souls at 1 piastre a day, equal to 300,000 piastres—that is, by month, equal to 9,000,000 piastres, and for fourteen months, equal to 120,000,000 piastres, or (the Turkish pound at 110 piastres) £1,100,000; deduct children in arms and mortality 101,000, leaving total expense £1,000,000.'"*

In plain English, after ravaging the district, the insurgents ask £2,000,000, a concession of one-third of the land of the lawful owners of the soil, with

---

* See "Affairs of Turkey," No. III., pp. 55, 56, 59, and 70.

certain other privileges, for relieving the Sultan of one of his provinces.

Count Andrassy and the other Russian diplomats were inclined to endorse those claims of the insurgents, but abandoned the idea when it was discovered that *the Turk had not got the money* to pay for them.

It may be some consolation to the reader to know that where the Panslavists, Turkey, and the Great Powers failed, people of genius made their appearance. Karageorgevich, ex-Prince of Servia, called upon all Slavs to unfurl the banner of their emancipation on the plain of Kossowa, where the battle was fought which resulted in the conquest of Servia by the Turks. The Prince is evidently affiliated either with the Western branch of the Internationalists or with the Nihilists, the Russian branch of the same organisation, for he distributed some thousands of medals with his own effigy on one side, and on the reverse, " Liberty, Fraternity, and Equality." This, however, was too much for Count Andrassy, who soon called him to order.

Equally unfortunate was a revolutionary hen, Mdlle. Merkus, who accompanied by the insurgent chief, Ljubibratics, took the field attired in Herzegovinian male costume. Why this lady was not suited to the sphere of action, our Consuls do not inform us. Consul Brock, however, gives the following account of her arrival at Trieste :—

" When off the port the vessel was boarded by a

commissary of police in a small steamboat, into which the party was removed and conveyed to the railway station. The chief, with his wife and Mdlle. Merkus, were then placed in a railway carriage attached to a goods train, which immediately left for Nabresina.

"An immense concourse of sympathisers awaited the arrival of the steamer, and loudly expressed their feelings of annoyance and disappointment on the removal of the party by the police; but a large number succeeded in reaching the railway station before the departure of the train, and, notwithstanding the presence of a numerous police force, made an enthusiastic demonstration of sympathy, with cries of 'Zivio' and 'Viva Italia.'"*

This lady, we believe, is Dutch by extraction, a philanthropist by nature, and a Republican by calling, and could not, therefore, be endured in the cutthroat company in which she had fallen, and hence was exported with the utmost expedition.

Where all others had failed, however, Slav genius took up the cause. As Byron says, "You'd best begin with truth, and when you've lost your labour, there's a sure market for imposture;" but, unfortunately, in this case there was no truth to begin with. And hence, writing from Ragusa, Consul Taylor forwards to Lord Derby a prospectus of a joint stock company, limited, which offered to take

---

* "Affairs of Turkey," No. III., page 47.

over the whole province of Herzegovina, consisting, as it did, of 220,000 square miles, and which they say " contains very fertile plains, valleys, fine watercourses, forests, and probably *rich mines which have never hitherto been examined.*" They will undertake to develop the resources of the country, and settle the whole matter for 1,000,000 francs. But, unfortunately for the originators of this brilliant scheme, the million francs were not forthcoming, and the country had been settled by being depopulated by the so-called insurgents.

The solution of the Eastern Question, then, according to the light of the Secret Societies, is: The Turks shall leave Europe, and give a few millions sterling for the privilege of being allowed to depart.

It is the demand of the banditti for ransom, only in this case he happens to have " caught a Tartar."

CHAPTER IV.

HAVE THE LIBERALS AN EASTERN POLICY?

ONE almost feels tempted, before giving a reply to this question, to ask whether such a thing as a Liberal party really does exist in England at the present time. Of course the Marquis of Hartington is supposed to be its leader; but who he is leading, and where he is leading them to, are, as Lord Dundreary says, "things that no fellar can understand." We all know there was a Liberal party once, that reckoned in its ranks some of our most eminent statesmen, and rendered noble services to the nation, for which their names will be honoured throughout all generations; but by some inscrutable decree of fate it was placed in the care of the "People's William," when, to use a printer's phrase, "it went into pie." The letters of the alphabet became suddenly fuddled, made words that could not be read, sentences that were unintelligible; it was, indeed, Babel—the confusion of tongues, as well as tempers, come back again.

Lord Beaconsfield, although satirical and amusing, is highly instructive. At the Guildhall Banquet, November 9th, 1876, he said that the principle and policy which had guided the Government during the last twelve months was that which had guided the most eminent statesmen in maintaining the peace of Europe, "among whom I will generously count those who preceded us in office."

The Liberals once had a policy on the Eastern Question. Have they one now?

We suppose that the following gentlemen may be reckoned among the leaders of the Liberal party—that is, supposing, as we before said, there is a party to lead, and that there is any place earthly or otherwise to which they can be conducted. We place Mr. Gladstone at the head, from his great talent and the position which he has always held in the nation, although, perhaps, we ought to have given that position to Lord Hartington, his nominal leader. Mr. Forster takes equal rank with either of them—is, indeed, better qualified to be a leader than a follower. It is exceedingly difficult to define what Mr. Lowe's position would have been by natural selection, since no order of nature that has ever yet existed could have been consonant with his. Lord Beaconsfield once said that in his Reform Bill he created a seat on purpose for the right hon. gentleman, knowing full well that he would ruin any ministry that he might be connected with;

and last, and *least*, His Grace the Duke of Argyll, who, in his flabby style, has been telling us " What the Turks are." We propose to devote a space to each of those gentlemen, and first of all Mr. Gladstone. He had been long hoping for an opportunity for attacking the Ministry, and especially his rival, Lord Beaconsfield. The time and circumstances seemed favourable, and at first appeared to promise success.

English public opinion, never very lucid upon matters relating to Turkey, became utterly confused and bewildered in consequence of the strange utterances of Mr. Gladstone and some of his followers. It is their habit to represent the Turk as a monster in human form, a Blue Beard in his household, a ruthless tyrant in the state, a cut-throat ready for any amount of brutality towards those not of his own creed. Even the good among them are represented by the ex-Prime Minister as "Monsters, so to speak, of virtue and intelligence."* In this confused state of the public mind, in reference to Turkey and her place in the European family of nations, the nation was shocked, and all its finer feelings outraged by reports of what had taken place in Eastern Europe.

The men who planned the " Bulgarian atrocities " —and they were planned and their effect anticipated, as we have already seen—selected the most appro-

---

* See " Bulgarian Horrors," p. 10.

priate time for throwing their sensational telegrams before the world. The "silly season" had set in with unusual severity. The sea serpent had been seen and accurately "done up" in the *Graphic* some time before the 12th of August, and the "Great Gooseberry" was a failure this year. Beyond this, the Liberal party, or we ought, perhaps, to say, the Radicals, were literally without a grievance. Mr. Cross was universally admitted to be a model Secretary of State for the Home Department, and, under his administration of those affairs, towns were being improved, and all matters of our social life well regulated. Lord Carnarvon, again, was uniting our Colonies and winning the highest fame a statesman can gain by consolidating our Empire. Lord Derby was, and is, the trusted Minister for Foreign Affairs; and, as for the Prime Minister, he had drawn the sting of Radicalism so adroitly that it was harmless as a "sucking dove." He had abolished the property qualifications for members of Parliament, brought about household suffrage with the lodger franchise, and vote by ballot, and sat there, supremely great, with a large majority behind him, like Neptune sailing o'er a calm sea.

It was in this calm, when the Radicals, like the famous Irishmen at Donnybrook Fair, were trailing their coats behind them and begging somebody to get up a row, that the Bulgarian horrors afforded an opportunity for an immense amount of writing and talking, most of it of the unprofitable order.

Mr. Gladstone led the way. The opportunity was too tempting, and he made a dash at the Government, and especially at the Prime Minister. All this was fair enough, so far as party warfare was concerned; but the right hon. gentleman goes out of his way, and, in order to damage his opponents, blackens by every epithet he can possibly make use of, and by a prostitution of the facts of history, the character of a great and noble race and a friendly Government who has always been our ally.

It is hardly possible, in the writings of any man who has ever made the least pretension to gentlemanly feelings, honour, or scholarly attainments, to find a more outrageous paragraph than the following:

"Let me endeavour very briefly to sketch, in the rudest outline, what the Turkish race was and what it is. It is not a question of Mahometanism simply, but Mahometanism compounded with the peculiar character of a race. They are not the mild Mahometans of India, nor the chivalrous Saladins of Syria, nor the cultured Moors of Spain. They were, upon the whole, from the black day when they first entered Europe, the one great anti-human specimen of humanity. Wherever they went a broad line of blood marked the track behind them, and, as far as their dominion reached, civilisation disappeared from view. They represented everywhere government by force, as opposed to government by law. For the guide of this life they had a relentless fatalism; for its reward hereafter, a sensual paradise." *

In his zeal against the Turk, Mr. Gladstone forgets that, as seen in history during the time that elapsed between the rise of Mohammedanism to the end of the sixteenth century, except in matters of faith, *the Moslems are always superior to the Christians.* He seems to appreciate fully the great blessings that Europe obtained from the residence of the cultured Moors in Spain, and ignores the fact that they and the Jews were driven from there with more than Bulgarian atrocities, and that *Te Deums* were chanted throughout Christendom in celebration of this unholy work. Even the monks of St. Albans, who had (according to the testimony of Archbishop Morton) converted a nunnery into a nest of courtesans for their own purpose, they, with their unholy lips, praised God for the victory of the Spaniards, and blessed the blood-stained hands of Torquemada. And they did this in a church, built in a style of architecture borrowed from the Moslems.

If the Turk, therefore, had been a cultured Moor, would he have been treated better by his Christian neighbours than his fellow-believer was in the Spanish Peninsula over three centuries ago?

---

* "Bulgarian Horrors and the Question of the East," p. 9.

Again he says, "They are not the mild Mahometans of India," of whom we suppose Nana Sahib and the butchers of Cawnpore are to be taken as specimens. "Nor," he goes on to say, "the chivalrous Saladins of Syria," a new race, we suppose, discovered by the right hon. gentleman, since they are unknown to science and history.

Now it would be easy to show that the fearful lies and accusations brought against the Moors and Jews in Spain, and other places, were as bad or even more monstrous than those that are at present advanced against the Turk. They were accused of worshipping demons, practising the "black arts," and slaughtering new-born babes, in their infernal rites. Indeed, there is no horror or infamy that the mind of man can conceive, or the body perpetrate, that was not published in pamphlets and preached from pulpits against those brave, innocent, and noble people.

Yes, Mr. Gladstone is right when he says, "In the olden time all Western Christendom sympathised with the resistance to the common enemy; and even during the hot and fierce struggles of the Reformation there were prayers, if I mistake not, offered up in the English churches for the success of the Emperor, the head of the Roman Catholic power and influences in his struggle, with the Turk." *

---

* "Bulgarian Horrors," p. 10.

These prayers were especially fervent in the reign of "Bloody Queen Mary," when the best, bravest, most noble and piously devout of England's sons and daughters were consigned to the dungeon, the rack, the headsman's block, the hangman's gallows, or the martyr's funereal pyre. Does the right hon. gentleman desire to restore the prayers, passions, and "Christian zeal" of those days, whose sun has set in agony and blood? Is he about to preach a "new crusade," as the *Russki Mir* is now doing?

It is painful at times to see how ridiculously wild, rabid, and unreasoning a man of Mr. Gladstone's abilities and position may become when the evil spirits of personal dislike and party zeal take possession of him. He quibbles, wrangles, and disputes over solemn treaties as though they were merely proof-sheets just come from the printer, sent on purpose to receive corrections and emendations; garbles, and so distorts Parliamentary documents, that it is hard to believe at times that the perversion is not intentional, and that he is not acting the part of a special pleader; and at other times talks the most wild and mischievous nonsense. Here is an example which has been before referred to. He says:—

"The case against Servia is the best part of the Turkish case. Servia, before she moved, had suffered no direct injury: she had no stateable cause of war. It does not follow that she has committed a wanton aggression, or has, in fact, been guilty of any moral offence."*

Unconsciously he has here given us a new definition of *Nothing*. A certain philosopher once said it was that thing from which everything had been abstracted: the Irishman defined it as a footless stocking without a leg, and in Cornwall they say it is an unborn pilchard without a ghost. Rochester wrote an elegant poem about it, and Byron also has some beautiful lines upon the same subject, but he makes nothing of it, and so falls back on "holding up the nothingness of life." Mr. Gladstone's is a non-stateable cause of war: *a cause of war* of which the brain of the most subtle diplomatist alive can form no conception, nor the voluble and lying tongue of the Serb give utterance to, and yet for which war may be declared without the aggressor being "guilty of any moral offence."

A declaration of war under any circumstances means wholesale destruction of human lives, the death of young men who are strong and brave, and an incalculable waste and destruction of property. public and private; it means the garments of the warrior dyed in blood; "the groan, the roll in dust, the all-white eye turned back within its socket." It means the tortures of the battle-field, where the demons, who wait on human agony, with fangs that know no pity, rend the wounded

---

* See "Bulgarian Horrors," p. 25.

until they are insane from pain; the hospital, with its painful surgical operations, and the life-long misery of the maimed; the tears of broken-hearted widows, wails from starving orphans —all this the victor has to endure: the vanquished has, in addition to all this, to mortgage the industry of the future to pay for the implements of destruction that ruined him.

That is war, at its best, and declared when circumstances have become so complicated that the knot cannot be untied, and nothing but the sword can cleave its way to the future. But the war which Mr. Gladstone wants to justify is war at its worst. It is a war of races and religions; a civil and a servile war. It is such a war as would be waged in Ireland if France and America were to adopt the cause of the Fenians—supply them with money and arms, and allow volunteer French officers to lead their armies. Neither the French nor Americans have any "stateable cause of war" against us; but would there be no "moral offence" in their entering into such a war, which would be as fierce as any that is likely to be waged in Servia or Bulgaria?

And after all, what is the right honourable gentleman's object? In his first pamphlet he was clear enough—the Turks were to be driven out of Europe, and if we were not exhorted to help in carrying out the work we were at least to give our sympathy and support to Russia while that Power did it, and encourage Austria to co-operate with her. This was tantamount to asking the nation to abandon its Eastern policy; admit that the Crimean war was a gigantic blunder, and that the time had come for the disruption of the Turkish Empire, whatever the consequences of that event might be. It seems also that we were in some mild way to render other help. One of his followers, Mr. Grant Duff, tells us what the ex-Premier's meaning is, for which explanation the present writer is thankful, since he has had great difficulty in making it out, except it be that Lord Beaconsfield and his party are the real Turks in Europe, and that it is only necessary for them to go out of Downing Street "bag and baggage" to set all things right again all over the world.

However, Mr. Grant Duff tells us what Mr. Gladstone's policy is. He says:—

"His proposals, omitting things about which every one is agreed, are twofold:—

"To stop, perhaps, the passage of troops from Asia to Europe—that is, to commit an act of war against Turkey. To remove the Turkish administration from Bosnia, Herzegovina, and Bulgaria."

All that is clear enough from the pamphlet, but by the time he had got upon Blackheath his valour had oozed from his fingers' ends, and he seemed to be in no way inclined to declare war against Turkey. He said a great deal about Bulgaria, but all with an eye to Downing Street. His anxiety now was that the Government should adopt his policy and carry it out, a course which would very soon have terminated their tenure of office, and have covered them with everlasting disgrace. In reality, the Bulgarian horrors had by that time become a valuable commodity as political capital, upon which a bankrupt party might hope to make a fresh start.

Fortunately, Mr. Gladstone has given us, on another occasion, what he kept back from his friends at Greenwich. In the *Daily Telegraph*, September 25th, 1876, there is a report of a speech delivered by him to some Liberals at Staindrop, Durham, where, being among his bosom friends, and having stipulated that there should be no reporters present, he makes a clean breast of it, and tells us what the Liberals ought to derive from their new Eastern policy.

The traitor, whoever he may be, who supplied the *Telegraph* with its report, informs us that the right hon. gentleman had been on a visit to the Duke of Cleveland at Raby Castle, and was engaged on Friday and Saturday in his favourite occupation of cutting down a large tree in Raby Park. A deputation from the Local Liberal Association waited upon him, and begged that he would favour them with an address. It was arranged that he should do so from his carriage on the way to view Staindrop Church. But rain coming on at the time, he was driven to the public hall, where he delivered a speech, amusing and also instructive, from the insight into his sentiments and aspirations which it affords us.

He commences by telling his audience that he hopes there will be no more meetings of the kind, "but when there comes to be a circle of these things, and with more or less speeches made here and there, although in good faith there is necessarily given the idea of some plot or intrigue going on to acquire notoriety." But he tells them, that such a reception makes a man forget his age and infirmities. "I assure you it is not always in such good trim and feather as I happen to be to-day." He then goes on to compliment the Liberals of Durham, who it appears were more loyal to their cause than others in the kingdom during the last general election. He desired, he continues, to avoid the Eastern Question, but was unable to do so, because the whole of the Liberal party and two-thirds of the Conservatives adopted his views. A statement, we suppose, which the right hon. gentleman would hardly repeat now.

"I have moved a great deal about England within the last few weeks, and come into contact with many thousands of men, and I have only found one single Liberal—and I hold up my finger for him—(laughter)—I have only found, I say, one single Liberal who was not heart and soul associated with this great national movement. (Loud cheers.) Under these circumstances what can be expected if the Liberal party wishes to carry its end into effect?

If the purposes of humanity and of justice in the State are amongst their ends, it is absolutely ridiculous and impossible for them to say that they will renounce, to carry their end to completion, all the aid of party. (Cheers.) I think we have given very fair terms to our opponents. What we have said to them, and I am quite sure we have cause for what we have said, is: 'There must be a change of policy; if you are really desirous that there should be no change of Government you will have to do your duty. (Loud and prolonged cheering.) We cannot stand the continuance of your policy on this question. That policy must go to the wall and go to the winds. (Renewed cheering.) We do not want you to go to the wall and go to the winds; but, if you will not change the policy, to the winds and to the wall you must go.' (Protracted cheers.) That is the long and the short of it. (Renewed cheers.) If I meet a Conservative friend, and my friend says to me, 'It is very unfair for you to turn this subject to the uses of party,' my answer is that his policy is clear, and I say, 'My dear friend, if you want to prevent the Liberal party deriving advantage as a party from the fact that a great question has arisen upon which we, as Liberals, are unanimous— (applause)—and upon which three-fourths of your side agree with them, whether they say it or not, your course is plain; go to your Government, speak more plainly to them than the Liberals, tell them you will have no nonsense about it, but that they must speak plainly, and think and act intelligibly.' (Cheers.)"

After continuing in this style for some time, he says:

"I think I could give for the information of your Conservative friends a perfect receipt. (Laughter.) I may say that for them—one which you may put in their hands, and which is as sure to answer its purpose as Holloway's pills. (Great laughter and cheers.) If they complain that your party is reaping an advantage from the discussion of this Eastern question, let their party take up the question with the same earnestness, the same enthusiasm, the same disposition—(cheers)—look straight to the end, and go straight towards it—(renewed cheering)—and then they will take the wind completely out of our sails—(laughter and cheers)—and I do say for one—speaking for myself —and I may, I feel sure, say the same for the Liberal party, that if they would take this course, I should be glad of it and perfectly content with it."

Nothing could be more apropos than the right hon. gentleman's simile—a quack medicine taken by a healthy man, would be as sensible as the Conservative party adopting his quack policy. It would act like the celebrated Pride's purge did on a former Parliament. We hope Mr. Holloway has been grateful enough to send the right hon. gentleman a supply of his pills for life. The advertisement certainly deserves it.

Our space forbids us to notice at much length either Mr. Lowe or the Duke of Argyll. The former on account of his almost rabid utterances, which have rendered everything he says of but little consequence; the latter because his speech is what Cobbett calls "wishey-washey." His grace brings an indictment against the Government and labours hard to convince the people of Glasgow that he is tearing their policy to tatters, and that they cannot possibly continue long in office. But in reality if his grace had thrown a handful of thistles into the Clyde they would have produced as much effect upon the great ocean as his pamphlet has upon the public life and policy of Great Britain.

The Liberal party then is divided, notwithstanding Mr. Gladstone's assurance that it is not, since neither Mr. Forster nor Lord Hartington adopt his views. He has made a great mistake of which we may suppose he is now conscious. It may be said of him, as Rogers said of the editor of the *Quarterly Review*, when he made a fierce attack upon Disraeli— "Croker tried to perpetrate a murder, and committed suicide." The Liberals cannot solve the Eastern Question, because they are themselves dissolved.

CHAPTER V.

OUR EASTERN POLICY.

The position of England in Asia may be easily defined. We want nothing, fear nothing, and will yield nothing to threats or coercion, at least until the battle is fought out and we are beaten, which will be a tough job for anyone who undertakes it.

Our policy is peace; our aim, mutual co-operation, with people of every nation, class, and creed. We covet no man's estate, nor anything that is his, unless we buy and pay for it honestly; seek no extension of territory, and having nearly one-fourth of the human race to govern, as it is do not wish to add to the population of our Empire, except it be when compelled by the simple order of Nature.

Our position, however, is held under certain conditions, which we must maintain at any cost.

The road to India, our Straits Settlements, China, Australia, New Zealand, and many other places, lies through Turkish territory. At present it is by water communication only; it must at no distant date be by rail. That railway, or at least a branch of it, must start from Constantinople, with a central station at Ispahan, a branch line to Teheran, the capital of Persia, the main trunk line passing by Herat through the Bolan Pass into India. Indeed, there is no possibility of our ever constructing or maintaining a railway to India except it be by the permission and cordial co-operation of the Ottoman Empire.

During the agitation that has just died away, the principal orators of which are, let us hope, ashamed of the part they took in it, many suggestions were made for coercing the Turkish Government; and, if I understand him aright, Mr. Gladstone contemplated at one time, not only our joining Russia in certain demands she was making on the Ottomans, but he intimates his readiness to go even farther than this—namely, that we should unite in a joint occupation of Turkish territory, which, if it means anything, means a declaration of war against the Sublime Porte.

Let us suppose that at a Cabinet Council, in which the right honourable gentleman had taken the chair, such a resolution had been arrived at. War with Turkey would then have to be proclaimed. The natural reply to that would be, the Suez Canal would be closed, in all probability filled up; all our telegraphic lines with India cut, and 40,000,000 of Her Majesty's subjects told that England had joined the Slav, the brigand, the cut-throat, who was bent on the destruction of Islam. "To your tents, O Israel!" would be a small affair in Judea to what would happen if the Sultan uttered words to the same effect from the mosque of St. Sophia. A people more numerous than the whole population of France would start into rebellion as soon as the intelligence reached them. The conviction would pass through the whole Mussulman world that they had no friend left but God. They would be at war with all the world that calls itself Christian, and outbreaks would take place more terrible in their consequences than a dozen Indian mutinies. At present Islam and England walk arm-in-arm, and care as little about the ravings of the Panslavists as for the howling of wolves in the Siberian deserts; but once let Islam stand alone, and the fate of both will be terrible.

It is impossible to exaggerate the trying position which Lord Derby has had to sustain since the first disturbances took place in Herzegovina. No one knew better than he did that the thing spoken was not the thing meant, and that the things done were intended to serve a purpose other than that which was professed. Hence the weariness which one feels has come over him in reading his despatches. He is sick at heart, and would, if possible, give up the whole affair. One day he is angry, disappointed, and weary at the helplessness or waywardness of the Turk, and the chaos which seemed for a time to reign at Constantinople. Then the lying and false pretences of the Montenegrin and Serb; the double dealing of Austria; the mendacious treachery of Russia. He is annoyed even with threats from Italy, and above all, with the cowardly and brutal outrages that were committed on all sides, and with the war, ostensibly conducted for one purpose, yet well known to have another in view. Professedly, it was a war of independence for liberating Christians from the government of the Mussulmans; in reality, it was to take Constantinople by surprise, the promoters of it well knowing that the little finger of Russia would be harder to bear than the whole hand of Turkey.

In his own policy Lord Derby was simply patriotic, resolute; in one word, English. He would never discuss the question of the integrity of the Turkish Empire, or the violation of the Treaty of Paris. If that celebrated document had to be rent to pieces, it must be by other hands than his, and on their heads would rest the responsibility. Hence he rejected the "ulterior" measures of the Berlin Memorandum; would not consent to the appearance of the united fleets of the guaranteeing Powers in the Bosphorus, and utterly repudiated all idea of a joint occupation of Turkish territory, even to the putting down of the rebellion. He writes to Sir H. Elliot to say, "Her Majesty's Government are of opinion that the Turkish Government should rely on her own resources to suppress the insurrection, and should deal with it as a local outbreak rather than give it international importance by appealing for support to other Powers."

He adopted the same policy with regard to the Servian war. In a despatch addressed to Lord A. Loftus, our Ambassador at St. Petersburg, and dated Foreign Office, July 1st, 1876,* he says:—

"The Russian Ambassador called to-day and asked me whether, in the event of war breaking out between Turkey and Servia, Her Majesty's Government intended, as he had been led to believe, to adhere to a policy of strict and absolute non-intervention.

"I said that such was undoubtedly the case, but that it must be clearly understood that Her Majesty's Government entered into no engagement to continue to abstain from intervention, in the event (which, however, I could not assume as probable) of a different course being pursued by other Powers."

In reality he always claims for England free and independent action, conscious of the vast interests which we have at stake; he is always careful not to commit himself to any course of action that would hamper our power to enforce our rights whenever an occasion might arise. He must at times have been sorely trying to the Turks, for he occasionally lectures

---

* See "Affairs of Turkey," No. III., pp. 351.

them in a style that must have tested to the utmost the amiability of our Eastern ally; and, on one occasion, he even went so far as to order our Ambassador to leave Constantinople and abandon the Turkish nation to its fate if his suggestions were not complied with. Contrasted with the conduct of Mr. Gladstone and his friends, more especially the Duke of Argyll, his despatches and other utterances stand in the same relation as the words of a wise and able statesman to the wrangling of shrews or ravings of demagogues.

One cannot help feeling that throughout the whole of these trying times, Turkey has not always been treated with the consideration due to an independent ally, and a great and generous people. If a concession is asked for it is always from the Turk. He is asked to pause in the midst of victory; to stand still when another step would give him success; with Belgrade in his grasp he is called upon to halt while Russia gains time to mobilise her army, place torpedoes at the mouth of her harbours, and fill Servia with "our volunteers," as the Emperor calls the soldiers of fortune, who are still swarming towards that place. The limits, however, of human patience have been reached at last. The Conference will assemble in a few days at Constantinople, and if it does nothing else—and those who best understand the matter to be discussed have little hope of peace being maintained by it—it will at least leave Panslavism and Islam eye to eye, foot to foot, and sword to sword.

When Isaiah, with his star-lit eyes, looked out upon the panorama of the future, One called, "Watchman, what of the night?" And he whose lips had been touched by a "live coal from the altar," said in response, "The morning cometh." Yes, and the morning will come again; but it is evening now, and the night is setting in in pitchy darkness. The sun of peace is sinking down in the Northern skies, and will not rise again for many a long, cold, and cruel day. The *aurora borealis*, which our forefathers considered to be flashings from the subterranean hell-fires of war, are already visible in the murky sky. Birds of evil omen, bearing lying despatches are flying from one capital to another, and the wolves and bears are falling into rank ready to pounce upon their prey.

And the intended victim is waiting for them. Like some noble bloodhound who scents the approaching wolf, crouches on the ground, gathers in all his energies, and waits with bated breath and muscles strung to the utmost tension the approach of the foe; so the Turk, with his hand on his sabre, keeps watch by the banks of the Danube: he may, and willingly will, perish, if Allah has so decreed, but he dies in the light of day, with the blood of the Slav streaming from his sword.

But will he die? If gambling were a Christian

virtue instead of a Mussulman vice, I would bet my life on the success of the Turk. Let him battle with the Slav in a fair and free field and he will come out victor. Turkey is in the same position now that England was on the accession of Queen Elizabeth. An able and resolute sovereign succeeded to the throne from which a half-crazed and impotent ruler had disappeared. There was discontent at home and an almost world-wide conspiracy abroad. Spain, the Russia of three centuries ago, talked with as much confidence then of disposing of the English as the Russians speak now of spoiling the Turks. But they failed. And their failure arose from the same cause as that of the Slavs will. An old, conceited, and arrogant race, brutalised by its victories over the weaker people of the New World and the feeble nations of Holland and Belgium, and Italy, cast itself upon the young English athlete. Viewed from a distance, the little ships of Hawkins and Drake seemed to have no chance against the "San Martino" and other floating castles which formed the Armada that came up the Channel; but in the death grip the gigantic galleon was almost helpless. It will be the same with Russia. Her conquests over the feeble peoples of Central Asia, and the Poles, have inflamed her vanity, but added nothing to her strength. She has a different antagonist to grapple with when she meets the fresh, daring young Turk. It will cost Russia two hundred thousand men to reach the passes of the Balkans, and double that number to pass them—if she ever gets there; and Constantinople will still be difficult to attain.

We may pause here, in order to glance at the relative positions of the two nations which will, in all probability, so soon close in a life and death struggle.

Russia has already been spoken of in Chapter I. of this book, and we have now to contrast her position with that of Turkey.

The difference between the two nations is as wide as the zenith and nadir. Race, religion, education—everything for which men live and strive in this world, and all they hope for and dread in the world to come, are essentially different with the two peoples.

The Turk is a member of the great brotherhood of Islam, a free man before Allah. To him all things are possible; the cobbler may drop his lapstone, and become a minister of state, provided only that God has given him the genius to fulfil the office. The present Grand Vizier was once a petty officer in the army. Indeed, there is hardly any country in the world—not even the United States of America—where genius is so much appreciated, and talent so liberally rewarded, as in Turkey.

The highest rank of nobility in that country is the Order of the Pen; and, that there should be a perennial supply of scholars, education among the Mussulmans is compulsory and universal. WHEREVER THERE IS A MOSQUE THERE IS A SCHOOL, and no child is allowed to grow up without some primary education and a knowledge, at least, of the principal doctrines of the Koran. Within the last quarter of a century much more than this has been attempted. Schools upon the best principle and models of Western Europe have been established; and little has been taught in England, Germany, and France that will not soon be imparted to the rising generation in every city, town, and vilayet of Turkey. The University of Constantinople has been founded under happy omens; and science and art applied to industrial pursuits will in no long time, let us hope, be as common in Asia Minor as in Western Europe.*

The dangers for Turkey lie neither in the internal relations of her Christian and Mussulman subjects, nor, indeed, in anything that Russia is likely to be able to do to her. In this instance, as Pliny says, "Fortune favours the brave." Panslavism has

---

* The following is a specimen of the almost senseless abuse heaped upon the Turks by the pro-Russian party in England. The special correspondent of the *Daily News*, writing from Philippoplis in a letter which appeared in that paper, November 13th, says:— "It will hardly be credited that the present Turkish Minister of Marine can neither read nor write! And yet such is the case." Anxious to know the truth upon this and some other similar matters, application was made to those in official position whose information could not fail to be accurate. The reply was, "Utter falsehoods."

thrown down the gauntlet, and Islam has taken it up. It matters little what the Conference now about to meet may decide. It cannot root out the ambition and antipathies of races. That will be solved by other means and at some distance from Constantinople.

The danger to England and her Statesmanship, as well as to Turkey, is that we should either allow, or take part in, any meddling with the internal affairs of the Ottoman Empire. Such a course of action would be productive of results similar to what would happen in Ireland if the Ultramontanes undertook the REFORM of the "*Green Isle*" under the supervision of foreign commissioners—a Fenian, let us say, from the United States of America; M. Villitoe, from France, who might remove the office of the *Univers* from Paris to Dublin; a Garibaldian from Italy; a Panslavist from Russia; and a disciple of Prince Bismarck from Germany,—Donnybrook Fair would be an earthly paradise in comparison with a country governed or *reformed* in this fashion.

IT WOULD BE A CASE OF BLOOD POISONING. Better far to cut off the diseased member at once, and have done with it. The body would lose something of its dimensions, but the vital current would remain pure, and the life and health be preserved. Turkish statesmen have pretty well made up their minds upon that matter, and the sooner our English politicians realise that fact, with all its consequences, so much better will they be able to assist in the solution of the Eastern difficulty.

Meanwhile, while writing this,* the Eastern Question is shrouded in darkness. In the words of the Koran, it is "As the darkness over a deep sea, billows riding upon billows below, and clouds above; one darkness on another darkness: when a man stretcheth forth his hand he is far from seeing it: he to whom God doth not grant light, no light at all hath he." †

---

* November 27, 1876.   † Sura XXIV., 40.

APPENDIX.

A.

It may be interesting to some of our readers to know what the precise condition of the Christians in Turkey was prior to those outbreaks which have so deeply agitated Western as well as Eastern Europe. Our Ambassadors and Consuls have always kept the English Government well informed upon the subject. Here are a few of their statements, to which scores of others of a similar character might, if necessary, be added:—

"To those who remember what Turkey was thirty or forty years ago, the improvement in the position of the Christians, and in particular the change in the bearing of the Sovereign and the high Ottoman functionaries, appear immense."—*Lord Lyon's Report to the Foreign Office, May 6, 1867.*

"With respect to religious freedom and toleration the Christian subjects have no cause for complaint.

A firman is, indeed, required for the erection of a new church, but so it is also for a new mosque, and it is granted, perhaps, with too much facility in either case. Bells are put up and rung, crosses and pictures carried about, and ecclesiastical dresses worn everywhere and openly."—*Consul Palgrave, Trebizonde.*

"Religious toleration on the part of the Government exists in a degree not equalled in all European communities."—*Consul Skene, Aleppo.*

"The inhabitants of these islands—the Sporades—who are all Christians, enjoy privileges which are quite unknown, not only in Turkey but in any other part of the world."—*Vice-Consul Billiotti, Rhodes.*

"I think it would be difficult to find many countries in which toleration is more largely practised, and in which the governing class allows its subjects more perfect enjoyment of their respective religions than in Turkey."—*Consul Blunt, Adrianople.*

"The condition of the Christians has immensely improved."—*Consul Rogers, Damascus.*

"All the Christians in Epirus, with the exception of a few foreigners, belong to the Greek Church. The places of worship are numerous, their services are frequent, and some of their ceremonies and processions attended with much display. But they are never interfered with in their religious exercises."—*Consul Stuart, Epirus.*

"When I first became acquainted with Turkey, more than thirty years ago, I could never have expected to see social equality realised to the extent it has been, and that in so short a period."—*Consul-General Longworth, Belgrade.*

"The Sultan wishing in his own person to set a conspicuous example of toleration to all his subjects, has recently adopted the unprecedented step of taking several Christians into the palace as domestic servants, who are placed on the same footing, and receive precisely the same treatment as his Mussulman attendants."—'*Levant Herald,*' June 14th, 1871.*

B.

When the *furor scribendi* seized Mr. Gladstone he decidedly "made a hit." He called the "spouters of stale sedition" from their obscure abodes, and they strutted their brief hour upon the stage. To use a familiar illustration, the whole affair went up like a rocket and came down like the stick. A journal that usually reflects public opinion with fidelity gives the following report of—

---

* See also "Modern Turkey," by J. Lewis Farley, pp. 178, 179.

THE MOST IMPORTANT MEETING YET.

The Three Tailors of Tooley Street met yesterday in as large a number as was possible, in order to discuss the position of the United Kingdom with regard to the East.

The meeting would have been held with closed doors, but there being only one door, it was considered superfluous to close it, particularly as no strangers showed any desire to come in.

The Second Tailor voted the First Tailor into the chair. This was immediately seconded by the Third Tailor, and carried by a very large majority.

The First Tailor said that he should have been most proud to have taken the chair, but unfortunately it had already been taken under a distress for last month's rent. (Loud cheers.) The proposed chairman went on to say that it would be quite in keeping with the object of the meeting, and with their professional capacity, if they were to sit cross-legged. (Great cheering, during which the meeting crossed their legs and took their seats.)

The first resolution was proposed by the Third Tailor, who said that he considered that all Turks should be exterminated. With that view he had already expunged Turkey from a map belonging to a friend of his, and hoped it might aid the cause materially. (Cheers.) He would move a resolution to the following effect :—

"That this meeting, comprising as it does the

principal inhabitants of the United Kingdom"—(hear, hear)—"would suggest to Her Majesty that all affairs of state should be at once committed to their charge, when probably a proper solution of the Eastern Question would be arrived at." (Loud cheers).

The resolution was carried by an overwhelming majority, the president giving his casting vote.

The Second Tailor thought that some pecuniary relief should be sent out to the sufferers—(hear, hear)—and that it should be done at once. (Great cheering.) He should, therefore, ask the president of the meeting to lend him a shilling; half of which he would pledge himself to spend in beer—(cheers)—and would promise to owe the other half to any honorary treasurer who might be appointed.

The President, after having re-crossed his legs, and remarked that he was in hourly expectation of letters of apology from all the Crowned Heads of Europe for not attending the meeting, went on to say that he fully concurred in what had been said. With regard to the shilling it was matter for consideration, and would probably take some weeks to decide. Nevertheless, he had no objection to other members of the meeting subscribing largely to the relief of the sufferers. (Murmurs.) Should Her Majesty decline to accede to their petition, they might take matters into their own hands. They surely ought to get *something* out of it. (Loud cheers.) He concluded with a fervent appeal to the

Second Tailor to stand something. This having been seconded by the Third Tailor, it was carried by an enthusiastic majority.

A somewhat warm discussion followed, after which the meeting uncrossed its legs and tossed for coppers till it dispersed.—*Punch*.

www.ingramcontent.com/pod-product-compliance
Lightning Source LLC
Chambersburg PA
CBHW022111230426
43672CB00008B/1342